GReAT LOve

(for Guys)

GREAT LOVE

(for Guys)

Truth for Teens
in Today's Sexy Culture

Aubrey Spears and Chandra Peele

new
hope
PUBLISHERS

Birmingham, Alabama

New Hope® Publishers
P. O. Box 12065
Birmingham, AL 35202-2065
www.newhopepublishers.com

Library of Congress Cataloging-in-Publication Data
Spears, Aubrey.
Great love (for guys) : truth for teens in today's sexy culture / Aubrey Spears and Chandra Peele.
p. cm.
ISBN 1-56309-965-9 (pbk.)
1.   Teenage boys-Religious life-Juvenile literature. 2. Sex-Religious aspects-Christianity-Juvenile literature. I. Peele, Chandra. II. Title.
BV4541.3.S68 2005
241'.66'08351--dc22
2005008104

All Scripture quotations, unless otherwise indicated, are taken from the New American Standard Bible®, Copyright © 1960, 1962, 1963, 1968, 1971, 1972, 1973, 1975, 1977, 1995 by The Lockman Foundation. Used by permission.

Scripture quotations marked (NLT) are taken from the *Holy Bible,* New Living Translation, copyright © 1996. Used by permission of Tyndale House Publishers, Inc., Wheaton, Illinois. All rights reserved.

Scripture quotations marked (ESV) are from The Holy Bible, English Standard Version, copyright © 2001 by Crossway Bibles, a division of Good News Publishers. Used by permission. All rights reserved.

Scripture quotations marked (*The Message*) are taken from *The Message* by Eugene H. Peterson. Copyright © 1993, 1994, 1995, 1996, 2000, 2001, 2002. Used by permission of NavPress Publishing Group."

Scripture quotations marked (NIV) are taken from the HOLY BIBLE, NEW INTERNATIONAL VER-SION®. NIV®. Copyright©1973, 1978, 1984 by International Bible Society. Used by permission of Zondervan. All rights reserved.

ISBN: 1-56309-965-9

N056130 • 0805 • 5.6M1

Dedication

To Lindsey and Holly:
As you walk through the battlefield
of life dodging arrows that send a
godless and worldly message,
I praise God you have chosen
His Truth to shield you.

—Chandra

To Janielle:
Knowing you and loving you
is my greatest joy on earth!

—Aubrey

Table of Contents

Acknowledgments

Aubrey I would like to thank Janielle, my wife, for your incredible sacrifice over the last two years as we wrote and rewrote *Great Love*. Your vision for this project not only preceded mine, it also sustained me in the countless all-night and all-weekend writing sessions.

Spencer, Sloane, and Silas—you are the greatest children in the world. Thanks for letting me spend so many hours behind the closed door of my basement office. When I look at you, play with you, and pray for you, I am reminded of why *Great Love* must be written.

Wayne and Nancy Spears—my parents; Myrt and Lou Richard—my grandparents; Mary and Dan Hickey—my wife's parents; Monica and Dale Pittman, and their children; Dee and Julie Spears; Bro. Chester and Mrs. Peggy; our church families—Holy Trinity Church, Cheltenham, England; Fairmont Park Baptist Church, La Porte, TX; Calvary Baptist Church, Bay City, TX.

Chandra I would like to express my deepest love and appreciation to Bruce, my husband, the love of my life. After nearly 25 years of marriage, I am most thankful for the great love you show me each day. You are my support, my love, and my inspiration to press on. This was especially true as I worked on *Great Love* in the solitude of my office day after day. Thank you, Bruce Peele, for the privilege of being your wife.

Lindsey and Holly—you make me so proud! Thank you for giving me the time I needed to write, but also for reminding me when it was time to stop! I love ministering to teens, but I love you so much more!

To Dorothy Nelson, my mom, and to my daddy, Joe Nelson, who is with Jesus—thank you for your godly example as you lived a life of great love together.

To Melissa and Danny, my sister and her husband—so happy that you have found great love in the Lord and in each other.

To Max Lucado, my friend and pastor—for your endless, amazing, anointed messages that keep me refreshed; and thanks also to Oak Hills Church, San Antonio, Texas. To Denalyn—even though we have months between our visits, your wise words keep me accountable to my family. Thank you! To Leslie—for your prayers, meals, and love for my family these past two years...you have in so many ways shown me the church. And to Carmen—what a blessing you are! You will never know how much your help in keeping my house clean means to me.

Both Chandra and Aubrey would like to thank the following people for their support, prayer, and contributions to this project: Dan and Alice Chappell, Butch and Kaye Daughtry, Dr. James and Beverly Drost, Neil and Linda Fuqua, Dr. Peter and Debbie Ledoux, Max and Denalyn Lucado, Mark and Brenda Minahan, David and Gail Morgan, Charles and Jeannie Pircher, Jim and Bianca Rhodes, Dr. Robert and Leslie Schultz, Bruce and Shirley Stein and the Stein Family, and Randall and Lenise Stephenson. Knowing you believed in the message and partnered with us in this cause, which we are so passionate about sharing, is greatly encouraging. Tom Cottar—for getting this project off the ground, "Thanks, man." Dee Spears, Eddie Landry, and Janielle Spears—for editing the book in the pre-New Hope stage. Rebecca England, our editor at New Hope—for your many helpful comments and expert direction. Tara Miller—for hours spent on cover design, "We love it!"

A special thanks to Rick Byargeon—when I [Aubrey] took a class from you on the book of Proverbs at New Orleans Baptist Theological Seminary in 1997, I was and continue to be deeply impressed by your expert exposition of this crucial part of Scripture. Your approach and insight forms the foundation for the material in weeks one and two.

Many of the devotional activities at the beginning and the end of each day were inspired by *Sacred Space: The Prayer Book 2005*, published by Ave Maria Press.

We also want to thank all the youth pastors who have already used the *Great Love* material and given such positive feedback. Powerful and practical...that seems to be the description most commonly used to describe *Great Love*.

Introduction

Sex is a great gift from a great God who loves you with a great love! The key to this entire study is this great love that God has for you. Listen in as the apostle Paul prays for the Christians in the city of Ephesus to understand the incredible love of God:

> *May your roots go down deep into the soil of God's marvelous love. And may you have the power to understand, as all God's people should, how wide, how long, how high, and how deep his love really is. May you experience the love of Christ, though it is so great you will never fully understand it. Then you will be filled with the fullness of life and power that comes from God.*
>
> —Ephesians 3:17–19 NLT

Did you catch that last line? The key to a full life is that you begin to understand the unbelievable love that God has for you. It is this *great love* that drives the Bible study you are beginning.

The Bible teaches that sex is one of God's greatest gifts to human beings. It is intended for the purposes of intimacy, pleasure, and making babies within the boundary of marriage. There's a problem, though. The devil, because of his wicked desire to destroy you, has saturated your culture with a devastating sexual immorality. Through a constant avalanche of perversion, he has convinced so many people that: (1) it is impossible to be sexually pure, (2) it isn't worth the sacrifice required to be sexually pure, and (3) the pleasures of sexual immorality that you can experience outside of marriage are good

13

enough to settle for. However, the truth of the matter is that Satan is really trying to create in you an ever-increasing craving for an ever-decreasing satisfaction. Ultimately he wants to leave you hurt, broken, and wallowing in your own misery.

But this is not God's desire at all. Every ounce of pleasure derived from sex outside of God's plan is only a hint of the pleasure that God offers when you live and love by His rules. As the architect, the inventor, the engineer of this gift, God knows how sex works best. It's His deal. It's His creation.

Do you want to experience great love in this life? Do you want to experience a great love life? Do you want something more than second-rate pleasures? Do you want all that God has for you? Do you want to honor God through your sexuality? Do you want to resist the temptations of this world? Do you want to please Jesus Christ, who died so that you could be saved? Then discover God's love. Let Him embrace you. That's the journey of *Great Love*! That's the journey that you are now beginning.

How To Use This Book

Welcome to *Great Love!* The information on this page will explain the basic format of this book.

Teenage guys and girls share some feelings and experiences in common, but they are also very different, especially when it comes to sex. Although both *Great Love (For Guys)* and *Great Love (For Girls)* have the same topics for the four weeks, the material inside is very different. The guys' book is written to and for guys, and the advice, stories, and examples inside focus on the realities of life for teenage guys. The girls' book is written to and for girls, and the advice, stories, and examples inside focus on the realities of life for teenage girls. Both authors, Aubrey and Chandra, developed and wrote both books together. But Aubrey took the lead in making the guys' book focused toward the guy side, and Chandra took the lead in making the girls' book especially helpful for girls.

If you decide to do *Great Love* as a small-group study, you can have separate groups for guys and girls, and then maybe let both groups come together for a debriefing and sharing time. Each book has a leader's guide in the back. Or a teenager can do the book as an individual study at home. If you choose to do this, we recommend that you get a friend or mentor to accompany you on this journey for help, accountability, and support (see *Hints* below).

Great Love is a four-week (or four-session) exploration of God's Word concerning sexual purity. The material for each week is divided into five daily studies. Use the remaining two days of the week to reflect, review, or catch up.

To do this, you will only need a Bible and a pen or pencil. For the first week you will probably need about 25-35 minutes per day to complete the material. The following weeks are more intensive, and will probably take about 35-45 minutes per day.

Each day begins and ends with a time of reflection and prayer that is designed to help you cultivate an awareness of God's presence and work in your life. Please do not rush through this part of *Great Love!*

pray

This icon is found whenever you are supposed to pause for reflection and prayer

read

This icon is found whenever you are supposed to read Scripture. Sometimes the passage will be in your book (either in the main body or in the margin of the page); other times you will need to read the passage from your own Bible.

The words will be in bold whenever you are given an activity that requires you to record an answer or draw something.

Hints:

- Discipline yourself to do *Great Love* at the same time and the same place (a favorite chair, or desk) every day.

- Do *Great Love* in the morning, before the day gets cluttered.

- Get a friend to do *Great Love* at the same time so that you can hold each other accountable to finish the material, and so that you can have someone to talk with concerning the things you are learning.

- Each week, pick a verse of Scripture from the study that you can memorize.

- Expect God to do something great!

How to Have Sex Before You Get Married

Introduction

Proverbs 7 tells you what to do if you want to have sex before you get married. Pretty crazy, huh? You gotta be thinking, *Why in the world would God tell me how to knock a home run with the ladies before I get married?* And you are right. God's plan is for you to say "No" to all sexual activity outside of marriage. But Proverbs 7 is one of those places in the Bible that will amaze you if you can really listen to what God is saying.

In the first two weeks of *Great Love* you will dig deep into this portion of Scripture and discover that God understands the pressures you are under when it comes to sexual temptation. He makes it clear in the beginning of the chapter (Proverbs 7:1–5) and the end of the chapter (Proverbs 7:22–27) that His plan is for you to have a great sex life with your wife. He created sex and intends for it to be a blessing within marriage.

Many teenagers have made commitments to abstain from sex until marriage, but there is a problem. While it is very good to make a commitment to abstinence by signing a card or praying a prayer, these things are definitely not enough. And that is what Proverbs 7 teaches. In the beginning of the chapter (Proverbs 7:1–5) you are challenged to make a firm commitment to be sexually pure. But in the remainder of the chapter you are taught that such a commitment requires more than your word, or your signature; it requires you to be wise in your actions.

That's why Proverbs 7:6–21 paints a vivid picture of what the path to sexual immorality looks like. Did you get that? The Scripture paints a vivid picture of the *path* that leads to sexual immorality. Why would the writer do this? So that you will check your own life and see if you are traveling down that road—willingly or accidentally. In other words, you need to examine your behavior, your habits, and your actions and see if you are taking the steps to sex before marriage. If you are, then you will be challenged to repent and choose the behaviors, habits, and actions that will lead you to sexual purity.

If you want to honor God through your sexuality, you must avoid all sexual activity until marriage. But that involves much more than saying "No" to intercourse. It means you must stay off the path that can and will lead you to making the mistakes that God is calling you to avoid.

Are you ready? If so, buckle your seatbelt and prepare for an exciting adventure in God's Holy Word.

Week One: Day One

pray

As you begin, dedicate this study to the Lord Jesus Christ. Offer yourself to God. Ask Him to use *Great Love* to rearrange your thinking so that it is in line with His will, to guide your feelings and desires so that they glorify Him. Ask Him to illumine your mind and your heart so that you understand and believe and delight in His plan for sexual purity.

Proverbs 7 is one of the great passages in the Bible on sexual morality. It's packed with very simple but life-changing truths. Through the author of this passage, God shares His plan for how to avoid sexual immorality.

read

Take a few moments to read all of Proverbs 7 from your own Bible.

In verse 1 you learn that this chapter contains the words of a very wise father talking to his son. He wants his son to be all that God has planned for him to be, and part of what this means is that he wants his son to be sexually pure. Yet the father knows that Satan will do whatever he can to seduce the boy into sexual sin.

It is significant that the father doesn't just tell his son, "Hey boy! Whatever you do, don't have sex until you get married!" In fact, there are plenty of places in the Bible in which you are simply told to be sexually pure (for instance, Galatians 5:19; 2 Timothy 2:22; Acts 15:20; 1 Corinthians 6:18; 1 Thessalonians 4:3), but in this passage there's a different approach. Instead of merely giving his son a command, the father paints a vivid picture that teaches the point in a creative, powerful, picturesque, and emotionally-charged way. You see, long before the days of TV and movies, God knew the power of strong visuals and an entertaining story. So here you are given a story, something to capture your imagination, to grab your attention, to haunt your senses so that you will grasp deeply the radically destructive nature of sexual sin.

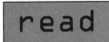

In order to really hear what this passage of Scripture is teaching, you must see and feel the danger of sexual sin. In the first two weeks of *Great Love,* you will dig into this amazing chapter of the Bible. For the first week you will focus on verses 6–21. This part of the story reveals how to have sex before you get married. In other words, Proverbs 7:6–21 exposes the tragic mistakes that a young man makes on the destructive path to sexual sin. For the second week you will focus on the beginning and the end of the chapter (verses 1–5 and verses 22–27). That section will reveal the commitments and the choices necessary for avoiding the mistakes that are highlighted in Week One.

Read Proverbs 7:6–7.
In these two verses you are introduced to one of two main characters in the story. How is he described?

`read`

_____

_____

_____

_____

pray

At the end of this week you will come back to these verses. For now, you need to know that this is a youth, a young man, someone to whom you can relate. Over the next few days you are going to discover the six basic steps that he took that guaranteed his sexual immorality. **Before you dive in, take a moment to pray. Dedicate your heart to God. Ask for the Holy Spirit to help you understand God's Word.** You could use these verses from Psalm 119 for part of your prayer. "Open my eyes, that I may behold wonderful things from Your law.... Make me understand the way of Your precepts, so I will meditate on Your wonders.... Teach me, O LORD, the way of Your statutes, and I shall observe it to the end. Give me understanding, that I may observe Your law and keep it with all my heart. Make me walk in the path of Your commandments, for I delight in it. Incline my heart to Your testimonies.... Turn away my eyes from looking at vanity, and revive me in Your ways" (Psalm 119:18, 27, 33–37).

Step 1: Go to the Wrong P_____

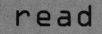

Read Proverbs 7:6–8. As you read, imagine in your mind that you are watching a movie. Picture what these verses describe. Think of the young man: what color hair does he have in your movie? What is he wearing? How old is he? Get a picture in your mind. Then re-read verses 6–8 very slowly, imagining the details.

Did you do it? Did you see the crowd of guys just hanging out? Can you hear the music? The jokes? The laughter? Can you smell the cologne? Maybe they were tossing a ball back and forth. Maybe they were arguing about their favorite football teams. And then, suddenly, one of the guys leaves the group. He walks around a few cars and then heads down the street. He knows where he's going, a man on a mission. Can you see him in your imagination? Can you see him check over his shoulder, just to make sure that none of his friends are following him? Where he's going, he wants to be alone.

In Proverbs 7:8 you find the first step to take in order to have sex or to fool around before you get married: **Go to the wrong place!** Fill in the blank at the beginning of this section, next to **Step 1**.

You will not go very deeply into this today, but you'll come back to it on Day Five. For now, spend the next few minutes in prayer using this simple exercise. Imagine that Jesus Christ is standing or sitting beside you. He's been there the whole time that you have been reading this book. He's been looking at you with love. He's been gently nudging your thoughts. **Now say to Him (out loud) whatever is in your heart, speaking as one friend to another.**

pray

Week One: Day Two

As you begin, remember that Jesus Christ is there beside you. He's gazing upon you with love. **Take just a moment to remind yourself of this, to thank God for His presence, to thank Him for the time that you are about to spend together.**

pray

read

Read Proverbs 7:1–27.

Yesterday you discovered the first of six steps that will lead to sexual immorality. What was that step? **Fill in the blanks.**

Step 1: Go to the W_____ P_____

Today you will look at steps two and three.

Step 2: Go There at the W_____ T_____

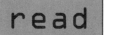

Read Proverbs 7:8–9.

What time of day it is when this guy goes to the wrong place?

_____

_____

_____

A literal translation of this verse tells you first that it is "twilight," then you are told that it is the "middle of the night," and finally you are told it is "in darkness." Can't you just picture this? Here's this guy walking out to his garage just as it is getting dark. He hops into his car, cranks it up, and pulls out of the driveway. He's cruising around town as the day slowly fades into night. It gradually gets darker and darker, and then, when it is pitch black, he pulls up to her house. Can you see this in your mind? Can you imagine it?

Why do you think this guy is going over to her house so late at night?

_____

_____

_____

_____

Have you ever noticed how easy it is to mess up at night? Why is sexual sin more common at night?

_____

_____

_____

_____

So the second step is: **Go There at the Wrong Time!** Fill in the blanks at the beginning of this section, next to **Step 2**.

Let's move on and discover the third step to fooling around and having sex before marriage.

Step 3: L_____

It takes two to tango. Up until now you've been learning about the guy. In verse 10 you begin to learn about the second character in the story—the girl. Read Proverbs 7:10, then use the space below to answer this question: **What you think is the first thing that this guy would have noticed about this girl?**

read

_____

_____

_____

_____

_____

_____

In our culture, prostitutes typically dress very sexy by wearing tight and revealing clothing. Why do they dress this way?

_____

_____

_____

_____

_____

_____

_____

_____

Did you write something about the fact that guys are turned on by things that they see? That the sight of a girl with tight and revealing clothes tempts guys to think about sex? **What types of fashions do girls wear today that cause you to notice and focus on their bodies?**

_____

_____

_____

_____

_____

Where do you go that you see girls dressed like this?

_____

_____

_____

_____

_____

read

To more fully understand what is going on in Proverbs 7:10, it will help you to hear something that Jesus said when He was teaching on the subject of sexual immorality. **Read Matthew 5:27–28.**

It's very important that you understand exactly what Jesus is and is not talking about when it comes to lust. Unfortunately, there is a lot of confusion on this subject. You may be a guy who is too easy on yourself, always excusing your behavior. Or maybe you are too hard on yourself, thinking that some things are sinful when in fact they are not. For example, there is a difference between lust and the temptation to lust. To see a girl and to be tempted to think sexually about her is not lust, but to cultivate that thought, to allow it to stay...that is lust.

Slowly read over the following definition of lust. *To lust is to think any kind of sexual thoughts about a person who is not your spouse.* This can involve many things, such as:

• focusing on a girl's breasts or her rear end

• imagining a girl naked, or picturing yourself watching her when she is naked

• imagining a girl having sex, or imagining yourself having sex with a girl

• imagining a girl in her underwear

In the space provided, write out the definition of lust (it's italicized above).

_____

_____

_____

_____

_____

Now read Matthew 5:29–30. Is Jesus being literal? Are you supposed to start cutting off the parts of your body that cause you to sin? I hear you saying, *Ouch! No way!* So why does Jesus go from talking about lust and adultery in verses 27–28 to talking about cutting things off in verses 29–30?

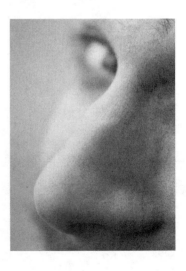

Jesus is using hyperbole. He is deliberately overstating the case, being extreme in order to illustrate His point. His point is that you need to declare war on lust. You need to take radical measures to avoid committing this sin. You need to remove yourself from all situations in which this sin presents itself. You need to hate this sin with a fiery and holy hatred.

What are some ways that you can declare war on lust in your life right now? For example, many teenage guys look at pornography on the Internet. Teenage guys (and grown men for that matter) should not have unhindered access to the Internet without someone holding them accountable. This person should be able to check the

history file and know that if it is empty that is not a good sign. Also, if you have access to the Internet in your own room this is very dangerous; you should seriously consider getting the computer out of your room.

The same thing goes for premium cable channels. Another area where guys should declare war on lust is the movies that they watch. Develop a habit of avoiding movies that produce lust (whether that includes full-blown sexual nudity, or merely innuendo). **In the space provided, record the ways that you can declare war on lust in your own life right now.**

_____

_____

_____

_____

_____

_____

So you've read a passage of Scripture where Jesus describes lust as a sin. In Proverbs 7:10 you are told that this woman is dressed like a prostitute. Are you beginning to get the picture? The third step to sexual immorality is **Lust!** Fill in the blank at the beginning of this section, next to **Step 3.**

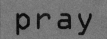

Spend the next few minutes in prayer. Once again, imagine that Jesus Christ is standing or sitting beside you. He's been there the whole time that you have been reading this book. He's been looking at you with love. He's been gently nudging your thoughts. What feelings have you experienced as you've worked through _Great Love_ today? With honesty share your feelings and thoughts with Jesus Christ. Say to him (out loud) whatever is in your heart, speaking as one friend to another.

As you begin, remember that Jesus Christ is there beside you, loving you. Take just a moment to remind yourself of this, to thank God for His presence, to thank Him for the time that you have spent together this week. **Now ask God for help, to be free from distractions, to be captured by Him. Ask God to focus your desires on Him.**

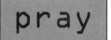

So far you have discovered three steps that lead to sexual immorality. Fill in the blanks.

Step 1: Go to the W_____ P_____

Step 2: Go There at the W_____ T_____

Step 3: L_____

Read Proverbs 7:1–27 slowly. Take your time with God's Word. Allow yourself to dwell on anything that stands out.

read

Today you will focus on step four.

Step 4: Flirt Like C_____

Read Proverbs 7:11–13.

read

In the first part of verse 13, what does the woman do when she sees the guy?

_____

_____

_____

_____

Read verses 11–12 again.

In the Hebrew culture this description of her "feet" was a metaphor for her genitalia. It means that this woman liked to show off her sexuality. She is extremely flirtatious with her body, dressing and acting in ways that cause you to notice her curves. She grabs the guy and lays a big kiss on him, sending off some serious "come and get me" vibes. The fourth step to immorality is **Flirt Like Crazy.** Fill in the blanks at the beginning of this section, next to **Step 4**.

Now be honest. Do you enjoy flirting? Hugging the ladies, having them sit on your lap, tickling, wrestling, hanging on each other? In Proverbs 7:11–13 you see that this type of behavior is a significant step on the road to sexual immorality. Many guys flirt with girls and act as if it is innocent. But you know that it can lead you to think sexual thoughts, to become aroused, to lust. Yesterday you learned that Jesus wants you to declare war on lust. Do you need to realize, and admit, that flirting that creates an atmosphere in which lust gets a foot in the door is always inappropriate?

With Step 3 you learned about the way Satan uses your eyes to get you aroused. Today you are learning that Satan also uses the sense of touch to get you in the mood. As a Christian you must make a commitment not to be flirtatious. You must be honest with yourself and your friends about how physical touch, even when it is innocent, can lead you down the road of fooling around before marriage. Even though it is commonplace in the world, and maybe even in your youth group, you must recognize that this is a serious step down the path of sexual immorality.

Read Proverbs 7:14–15. Before you finish today, there is one more thing that you should notice. This is difficult to understand if you are not familiar with the culture in which this passage of Scripture was written and originally read. If you were an Israelite living when this was written, it would have been very clear to you what is going on at this point in the story. You see, the picture is of someone who has just left a worship service where she offered praise to God in the form of a peace offering (see Leviticus 7:11–21).

　　　　Great Love for Guys

This was an offering someone took to the temple and presented to God as a way of expressing joy and thanks for God's presence in her life. One third of the sacrifice was burned up on the altar, another third of the sacrifice was given to the priest who presided over the offering, and the final third of the sacrifice was taken home by the person who brought the offering. Now, this person was supposed to go to her house and eat that portion of the offering as an act of worship. Furthermore, she was supposed to eat it with someone else. You were not allowed to eat this part of the sacrifice alone.

So this woman is saying to the young man, "Hey, I've just been to worship. I presented a peace offering. You know what that means don't you? It means that I'm not finished worshiping. It means that I've got a nice cut of meat and I'm supposed to eat it with someone else. Why don't you join me for this meal?" Do you see it? Do you see what she is doing? She is using the worship of God as an excuse for a sexual affair. How much more perverse can she be? But aren't there many teenagers who do the same thing today? They use church to hook up. Some guys are really good at talking a good game spiritually in order to impress people enough to drop their guard. But their real motivation is picking up the ladies. Are you like this?

Spend the next few minutes in prayer. Once again, imagine that Jesus Christ is standing or sitting beside you. Be honest. How are you reacting to this material? Are you comforted? Confused? Challenged? Angry? Cold? Indifferent? Scared? Sad? With honesty share your feelings and thoughts with Jesus Christ. Say to him (out loud) whatever is in your heart, speaking like you would to a trusted friend.

Week One: Day Four

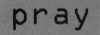

pray

As you begin, think about the fact that Jesus Christ has been here waiting for you. He wants to spend time with you, even more than your very best friend does. **Take a moment to greet your loving Lord.** Since God loves you unconditionally, you can afford to be absolutely honest with Him. In God's loving presence, unwind the past twenty-four hours. Start from right now, and look back moment by moment. As you do this, thank God for all of the goodness, and seek forgiveness and healing for the wrong.

read

Read through Proverbs 7:1–27 once again, listening closely for God's voice.

Today you will explore the fifth and sixth steps down the path of sexual immorality.

Step 5: T_____ About S_____

read

Read Proverbs 7:16–18.

In verses 16–17, what is she describing?

_____

_____

_____

_____

_____

She is talking about her bedroom, her couch, her bed. This lady is wealthy—so she has the finest imported linens to have sex on.

Read verse 18. Can you hear the woman? She's saying, "Hey big boy, this is going to be good. We'll do things you've never imagined. We're going to feast tonight, and guess what: I'm the main course!" Verses 16–18 show, in graphic detail, another step along the way to having sex before you get married. The fifth step is to **Talk About Sex!** Fill in the blanks at the beginning of this section, next to **Step 5**.

read

In Step 3 you learned that Satan uses your eyes to get you aroused. In Step 4 you saw that Satan uses your sense of touch to get you aroused. Now you are learning that Satan uses your ears. He uses the sense of hearing to get you in the mood. Isn't it amazing that this passage of Holy Scripture was written thousands of years ago, and yet Satan is still operating in the same way today? **Fill in the space below with the names of places and occasions where you hear talk that is about sex.** For example: music, movies, lunchroom, locker room, jokes. Be sure to include things you read that talk about sex, like magazines, books, billboards, or advertisements in the mall.

_____

_____

_____

_____

Let's look at the final step.

Step 6: G_____ A_____

Read verses 19–20.

read

In these verses the lady is saying, "Oh, in case you're wondering, my husband is gone for a whole month. We don't have to worry about getting caught. You won't need to hide under the bed. We've got the house to ourselves. There is no danger. Baby, this is your dream come true."

The sixth step is simple: **Get Alone!** Fill in the blanks at the beginning of this section, next to **Step 6**.

This brings you back to the very first step, doesn't it? Remember Step 1? Go to the wrong place. You see, teenagers usually don't have sex when their parents are in the room with them! Most sex outside of marriage occurs when a couple feels safe from getting caught. **What are some places and situations where teenagers can typically find themselves alone and facing the strong temptation of engaging in sexual immorality?**

_____

_____

_____

_____

_____

read **Read Proverbs 7:21.** Here you see that the woman successfully seduces the guy. But you already knew that—you already knew that the guy was a goner! There was no chance that he was going to resist. He had already gone too far down the path. He had already taken too many steps in the direction of sexual immorality.

What are the six steps that lead to her bedroom? Can you remember them? Try to fill in the blanks without looking up the answers.

Step 1: Go to the _____ _____
Step 2: Go there at the _____ _____
Step 3: _____
Step 4: _____ like _____
Step 5: _____ about _____
Step 6: Get _____

Spend the next few minutes in prayer. Imagine that Jesus Christ is standing or sitting beside you. Now, slowly, in God's presence, review the six steps that God has shown you which lead to sexual immorality. As you do this, confess to God concerning any of the steps that you are taking. Ask Him for the grace to let go of your worries and fears and guilt. Ask Him to help you to be open to what He is asking of you.

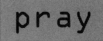

Week One: Day Five

As you begin, think about this image. Saint Ignatius once remarked that a bland and shapeless tree trunk could never believe that it could be sculpted into a beautiful statue. And if it had the choice, that tree trunk would certainly never submit to the chisel of the artist. Just as that artist can see what the tree trunk is *and* what the tree trunk can become, so God sees you. Your loving Creator sees what you are and He sees what you can become. Ask God for the grace to surrender to His shaping.

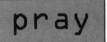

Again, read slowly through Proverbs 7:1–27. Be sure to listen for God's voice. Pay attention to anything that strikes you.

Go back and look at verses 6–7. What stands out about this guy in verse 7?

_____

_____

_____

_____

_____

If your right eye makes you stumble, tear it out and throw it from you; for it is better for you to lose one of the parts of your body, than for your whole body to be thrown into hell. If your right hand makes you stumble, cut it off and throw it from you; for it is better for you to lose one of the parts of your body, than for your whole body to go into hell.
—Matthew 5:29–30

He's naïve and simple. He lacks common sense. You see, you don't have to be brilliant or beautiful to have sex outside of marriage. You just have to make the mistakes that you've been learning about over the past few days. That's right. The primary characteristic of this young man was the fact that he could not tell the difference between reasonable and unreasonable choices, between dangerous and safe actions. He couldn't tell that he was making choices that were going to ruin his life.

In Proverbs 7:6–21 God exposes six extremely common steps that Satan uses to lead you down the destructive path to sexual immorality. Each of these steps is a step into a minefield, and the best way to avoid being destroyed by a mine is to stay out of the minefield.

Read over the list of six steps and put a mark beside the steps that you know you are already taking. Be honest with yourself. Mark the steps that are already present in your life.

Step 1: Go to the Wrong Place
Step 2: Go There at the Wrong Time
Step 3: Lust
Step 4: Flirt Like Crazy
Step 5: Talk About Sex
Step 6: Get Alone

In the space provided below, write some practical changes that you can make to remove these steps from you life. But first, remember Matthew 5:29–30. Remember that you must be ruthlessly radical in your effort to rid your life of these the dangers.

_____

_____

_____

_____

Are you ready for a big challenge? If you are serious about avoiding these six deadly steps, then find a friend who has the same commitment and confess to him what you marked and the changes that you need to make. (This friend should be a guy. Sharing these things with a girl could result in the very temptation that you are trying to avoid.) Ask your friend to commit to praying for you on a regular basis, and to holding you accountable for making these changes.

In your closing prayer time, do things a little differ-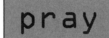
ent today. **Take the next few moments to write a prayer of response that focuses on how God has spoken to you through** *Great Love* **this week.** An example is below. Maybe you will write this one out and personalize it as your own prayer, or maybe you will write a completely different prayer about one of the other six steps to sexual immorality that you struggle with.

Dear Heavenly Father,
Thank You for Your Word. Thank You for painting such a graphic picture of the path to sexual immorality. Instill in me the desire to avoid this deadly road. When I am lusting, change my heart and pursue me until I recognize it. Lord Jesus Christ, I know that nothing I do or don't do will cause You to love me more or less. Thank You for loving me the way I am and for loving me enough to keep putting the pressure on me so that I don't stay the way I am. Continue to teach me through Your written Word how to be more like You. Help me, Lord, to be more like You.

In Jesus Christ's name,
Amen.

_____

_____

_____

_____

How to Avoid Having Sex Before You Get Married

Introduction

Proverbs 7 is full of surprises. You saw this last week, with the vivid story of the young man who traveled down the perilous path to sexual immorality. Perhaps you discovered that even though you desire to be sexually pure, the truth of the matter is that you have begun the treacherous journey yourself. Or maybe you've done more than begin the journey, you've reached the end. You've fooled around, had sex, gotten involved in pornography, or allowed lust to run freely through your thoughts and imagination. On the other hand, you may have realized that you have not taken a single step in the direction of that dangerous road. But being aware of the route will help you avoid it in the future.

What you saw, felt, experienced, and learned last week was just the beginning of *Great Love.* It's not enough simply to show the road to immorality; much more than an awareness of danger is required for you to remain pure before the Lord. This week, you'll go back to Proverbs 7 to find God's plan for avoiding the traps and temptations that this world assaults you with on a daily basis.

God wants you to experience His great love in every area of your life, including your sexuality. So this week will focus on the beginning (verses 1–5) and the end (verses 22–27) of Proverbs 7. The first few days will lead you to discover how God wants you to treat His plan. The last few days will explore exactly what God's plan is for resisting the devastating counterfeit pleasures of Satan's path.

Week Two: Day One

The Most Important Decision of *Great Love*

pray

Maybe your last few days have been great, or maybe your life has been terrible. Either way, slow down and dwell on (focus on or think about) God's presence around you and within you at this exact moment. Remember, He's here and His heart is full of love as He gazes at you right now. **Now ask God to shine the light of His Holy Spirit in your mind so that you will understand His Word, and to illumine your heart with His Holy Spirit so that you will delight in and trust His Word.**

read

Return to Proverbs 7:1–27 and once again read it slowly. Take your time. This is God's Word, so listen closely for His Holy Spirit gently nudging your thoughts. Dwell on anything that stands out to you.

W_____ I A_____ G_____

Plan for A_____ Sexual Immorality?

Read Proverbs 7:1–5 (it's in the margin of this page).

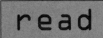

In verses 1–2, what three things does the father specifically command his son to "keep" or to "treasure"? (Fill in the blanks.)

My W_____
My C_____
My T_____

When the father challenges the son to keep "my words," "my commandments," and "my teaching," he is using phrases that are very common throughout the Old Testament in describing God's law. In fact, the people who originally read this passage of Scripture (when it was first written) would have immediately recognized these phrases as ways of describing God's law. This means that the father isn't merely giving his son human advice. He's actually giving his son God's advice. The plan that you are about to learn is not something that this father just made up; it is *God's* plan for resisting sexual immorality.

Therefore, you are faced with a choice. Not just any old choice, but the most important choice of the entire book. If you want to honor God in your sexuality, if you want to resist the sexual immorality that Satan will tempt you with, if you want to be sexually pure, then you must choose to accept God's plan. **This is the most important decision that you will face in *Great Love*! Will you trust God enough to accept His plan for avoiding sexual immorality?** The challenge in Proverbs 7:1–5 is to settle this issue in your heart, to make up your mind that you will trust God's Word—even when you don't understand, even when you don't like it, even when you disagree and think that you have a better idea. This is the whole focus of today's session. It all boils down to one question: Will you accept God's plan or not? There really is nothing in *Great Love* that is more important than this!

¹My son, keep my words and treasure my commandments within you. ²Keep my commandments and you will live, and my teaching as the apple of your eye. ³Bind them upon your fingers and write them upon the tablet of your heart. ⁴Say to wisdom, "You are my sister," and call understanding, "My wife," ⁵ because they will keep you from the adulterous woman, from the prostitute with her seductive words.

—Proverbs 7:1–5 (author's paraphrase)

Fill in the blanks at the beginning of this section with the appropriate words: *Will I Accept God's Plan for Avoiding Sexual Immorality?* At the end of this week you will have a chance to record your answer to the question. In order to prepare for that moment, the next few days will help you dig deep into Scripture, to experience God's presence, and to receive God's grace as you consider the most important decision of the entire study.

read

Read Proverbs 7:1–5 again; this time circle every occurrence of the word "keep."

Did you locate three occurrences? In the first two verses the word is used twice. Here it is a command (an imperative). The father is telling his son what to do. It's kind of like a coach telling you to run extra laps. Maybe your coach is making a suggestion or a request, but sometimes (and you can tell when this is the case by the tone of his voice) your coach is not giving you an option; it's a command, an order. When the word "keep" is used in Proverbs 7:1–2, the father is commanding the son to keep God's plan.

In verse 5 it is different. Do you see that the same word ("keep") is used, but it is no longer the father telling the son what to do? Here the word ("keep") is not in the form of a command. This time the father is not telling the son what to do with God's plan; instead the father is explaining what God's plan will do for the son. It's a play on words: "You *keep* God's plan, and God's plan will *keep* you." In other words, you keep God's plan (by obeying it) and God's plan will keep you (by protecting you). God's plan will be like a bodyguard or body armor against sexual immorality. It will guard you, it will protect you, it will help you avoid the trap of sexual sin. **In the space provided below, list some of the specific temptations to sexual immorality that you need protection from at this stage in your life.**

_____

_____

Isn't it great to think of God's plan as a bodyguard against these temptations? Now it's time to dig deeper. There's more here that will help you understand the decision you're facing. When you keep God's plan for avoiding sexual immorality, you get more than protection from sexual sin. **Go back to Proverbs 7:1–5 recorded in the margin. Read verse 2 again.**

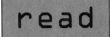

What does it say is a result of choosing God's path?

_____

_____

_____

_____

_____

So verse 5 teaches that God's plan works; it keeps you from sexual immorality. And verse 2 teaches that "you will live." This doesn't mean that you will simply get to keep on breathing. It isn't so much talking about the _length_ of your life as it is talking about the _quality_ of your life. This is a huge deal. In fact, it is one of the most important themes in the entire Bible. When you follow God's plan, life is good. God will fill your soul with pleasure, delight, joy, and satisfaction. Listen to this incredible verse that describes God as the source of pleasure: "In Your right hand there are pleasures forever" (Psalm 16:11). You see, this plan that God offers you, it isn't a cruel trick to deny you pleasure, or good feelings, or fun times. God passionately desires for you to live life to the fullest (John 10:10), but only His plan, only living life God's way, will guarantee that you live a life of awesome satisfaction and extreme pleasure. Accepting God's plan to avoid sexual immorality is really about accepting God's plan for _abundant life_!

This idea of "the good life" does not mean that you will never experience pain and suffering. In fact, the Bible is very clear that suffering is part of your growth in Christ. Suffering is often God's invitation to intimacy; it is something that God uses in your life for His own glory (for example, James 1:2–4, Philippians 3:10–11, Hebrews 5:8, etc.). It is clear that a balanced biblical view emphasizes God's desire to bless while holding forth the mystery of suffering as part of that blessing. And yet, this entire study is based upon the balanced teachings of Scripture that sex is a gift from God and part of the beauty of that gift is that God intends it to be intensely pleasurable. After all, there is an entire book in the Bible devoted to the exhilarating pleasure of sex within the confines of marriage (Song of Solomon).

pray

Bless the LORD, O my soul, and all that is within me, bless His holy name. Bless the LORD, O my soul, and forget none of His benefits; who pardons all your iniquities, who heals all your diseases; who redeems your life from the pit, who crowns you with lovingkindness and compassion; who satisfies your [desire] with good things, so that your youth is renewed like the eagle.
—Psalm 103:1–5

For the next few moments, imagine that Jesus is standing or sitting across from you. What is stirring in you? What feelings are you experiencing? What thoughts are going through your mind? Honestly share these things with Jesus, the lover of your soul.

Psalm 103 is an exciting command to bless God by reminding yourself of all that He does for you. In the final moments, make these few verses into your own personal prayer of worship. And don't forget to bless God by telling Him "Thanks" for the good gift of pleasure and sex.

Great Love for Guys

How Do I Treat God's Plan? (Part 1)

As you sit there, God is with you. He is all around you and within you. He hears every beat of your heart, every breath. He knows all that you think and all that you feel. He's aware of everything about you because He loves you beyond anything you can imagine. **Sitting there, in His presence, look honestly at your feelings over the last day. Consciously rewind the last twenty-four hours, the instances of excitement and sadness, confidence and fear, your successes and failures. As you do this, acknowledge the moments of God's intimate presence in your life. Thank Him.**

pray

Read Proverbs 7:1–27. Dwell on anything that may stand out to you.

read

Yesterday you were challenged to accept God's plan for avoiding sexual immorality. At the end of this week's study, you'll have a chance to record your decision as to whether you'll accept that challenge or not. But what exactly is God's plan? The answer to that question will have to wait until the last two studies of this week. In the meantime, Proverbs 7:1–5 has more to offer. You see, the details of God's plan for avoiding sexual immorality are not given until the final few verses of the chapter (Proverbs 7:22–27). Before getting there, God wants to be very clear about how you should handle His plan once you do receive it. So today and tomorrow you will focus on verses 1–5, where you learn how to treat God's plan for avoiding sexual immorality. Then, on Thursday and Friday you will learn the details of His plan.

T_____ it! (Proverbs 7:1–2)

[1] My son, keep my words and treasure my commandments within you. [2] Keep my commandments and you will live, and my teaching as the apple of your eye. [3] Bind them upon your fingers and write them upon the tablet of your heart. [4] Say to wisdom, "You are my sister," and call understanding, "My wife," [5] because they will keep you from the adulterous woman, from the prostitute with her seductive words.
—Proverbs 7:1–5
(author's paraphrase)

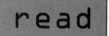 **Read Proverbs 7:1–2.**

The Old Testament was originally written in Hebrew. In Hebrew, one of the ways you could write poetry was to use lots of synonyms. This is what's going on in Proverbs 7:1–2. The second phrase of each verse is actually a synonym of the first phrase of each verse. Look at this diagram.

verse 1: Keep my words → treasure my commandments
verse 2: Keep my commandments → as the apple of your eye

Do you see how the last phrase of the first verse, "treasure my commandments within you," is a synonym for the first phrase of that same verse, "keep my words"? And the last phrase of the second verse, "as the apple of your eye," means pretty much the same thing as the first phrase of that verse, "keep my commandments." In other words, part of what it means to "keep" God's plan for sexual purity is that you "treasure" it, and you treat it like "the apple of your eye."

What are some things that you treasure?

_____

_____

_____

_____

What are some practical actions you do that prove you treasure these things?

_____

_____

_____

_____

Maybe you treasure a car, or a shirt, or your hair, or your athletic ability, or a relationship, or your grades and class ranking. These are things that you consider very precious. You protect them from being stolen, or lost, or taken from you. You take care of them. In the same way God is calling you to consider His commands, His plan for avoiding sexual immorality, as very precious. He wants you to realize that this plan is a gift. Out of His grace and kindness, He is making known to you the solution to sexual pressure and temptation. What an amazing gift! It is something you should honor, cherish, and love.

Ironically, many people treat His plan in the opposite way: they hate it and despise it. They think it is silly, stupid, and old-fashioned. They think it is not something that will work in a complex, pressure-filled, sex-filled, postmodern world. But God, on the other hand, is challenging you to regard His plan as a treasure. Even before you know what the plan is, He is telling you how to treat it once you discover it. Fill in the blank at the beginning of this section with the appropriate word: **Treasure it!**

Now what exactly does God mean when He tells you to treasure His plan? The last phrase of Proverbs 7:2 is translated in this book as "apple of your eye." That's the key to the answer. In the original language of the Old Testament (Hebrew) the literal translation is "pupil of your eye." In the margin there is another verse (Deuteronomy 32:10) from the Old Testament where this same phrase is used. **Read this verse and then use the space below to record what you think it means to treat something "as the pupil of your eye."**

He found him in a land of desert, and in a howling wasteland. He surrounded him, He cared for him, He guarded him as the pupil of His eye.
—Deuteronomy 32:10 (author's paraphrase)

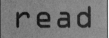

_____

_____

_____

_____

_____

_____

You treat the pupil of your eye with extra special care. You guard it constantly, whether you are conscious of this or not. If the smallest amount of dust gets in your eye, you tear up and start blinking. You rub your eyes and wash them out, doing whatever is necessary to remove the tiniest particle. Think about what this means. Think about how careful you are to keep stuff from touching your eye. If you wear contact lenses, do you remember how hard it was to put the contacts in when you first got them? This is because you had to unlearn a very natural instinct—to keep things out of your eyes. *God is telling you to treasure His plan by protecting it like you protect your pupil.* You are supposed to have the same huge amount of concern for God's plan that you have for your own pupils.

Treat God's plan like a prized possession. Care for it, value it, enjoy it, and love it. Be very careful that you don't lose it, that you don't forget it. Too many people look at God's Word, at His plan, like medicine. They see it as something that is necessary but unpleasant. Instead, His plan is supposed to be something that you desire intensely, something that you are passionate about, something that puts a smile on your face. **Use the space below to list some ways that you can treasure God's plan.** Remember you are going to learn what this plan is on Thursday and Friday. For now, even before you know what it is, you are learning how to treat it.

_____

_____

_____

_____

_____

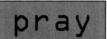

Yesterday you were encouraged to pray (at the beginning) for God to illumine your heart with His Holy Spirit so that you would delight in and trust His Word. Just because you understand the Word of God does not mean that you have received that Word by faith. To truly receive the Word it must take deep root in your heart, so that it can grow up and become a mighty fortress able to sustain you and repel all the assaults of temptation. **Conclude your time today by asking God to give you a passionate delight in His plan so that you can honestly treasure it.**

Week Two: Day Three

How Do I Keep God's Plan? (Part 2)

Romans 8:14 explains that God's children are led by God's Spirit. As you mature in your walk with Christ, you grow to be increasingly sensitive to the presence and the leading of the Holy Spirit. Elizabeth Barrett Browning wrote: "Earth is crammed with heaven, and every common bush afire with God; but only he who sees takes off his shoes." Take a moment to dwell on the presence of God around you. Where in your life do you see God's activity? **Praise Him for this generous gift of His presence.**

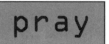

All who are led by the Spirit of God are sons of God.
—Romans 8:14 (ESV)

On Day One of this week you were challenged to accept God's plan for avoiding sexual immorality. Yesterday you learned to treasure that plan like the pupil of your eye. Today you will continue to explore how God wants you to treat His plan.

Read Proverbs 7:1–27. Don't rush. Listen closely for God's voice speaking through this chapter of His Word to you today. Dwell on anything that catches your focus.

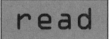

M_____ in it! (Proverbs 7:3)

Read Proverbs 7:1–5, focusing on verse 3.

read

While verse 3 sounds very strange today, it was not a strange saying to the people who originally heard these words in the times of the Old Testament. In fact, it was a fairly common saying. So when they heard "bind them upon your fingers" and "write them upon the tablet of your heart" they would have understood exactly what was meant. It meant that they should saturate their life with these principles, these commands, this plan. They should hang it up on the walls of their house, wear symbols of it on their fingers as rings. In other words, symbols of this plan were supposed to surround them, to be always before them, catching their eye. But also, it should be something they think about, talk about, and meditate on. In this way all of the external physical representations were supposed to aid in driving God's plan deep into their life, so that it took root in their heart. Proverbs 7:3, then, is another way that you should treat God's plan: **Marinate in it!** Fill in the blank with the appropriate word at the beginning of this section.

There are lots of ways that people symbolize and represent God's Word today. Some people wear Christian t-shirts or True Love Waits rings; some hang up posters with Scripture. These are good ways of carrying on the ancient tradition of outward symbols as one part of what it means to marinate in God's Word. What are some practical ways that *you* can symbolize and represent God's plan for avoiding sexual immorality? Be creative! **Record some ideas for how you will surround your life with God's plan so that you marinate in it.**

_____

_____

_____

_____

Are you an artist? You can paint, sculpt, or draw images that represent God's plan for sexual purity. You can write stories, poems, and songs, or create Web sites that remind you of this part of God's Word. By doing these things you are marinating in God's plan for avoiding sexual immorality.

L_____ it! (Proverbs 7:4)

Read Proverbs 7:1–5 again; this time focus on verse 4.

read

Here is a great summary of all that you've been learning so far this week. This short verse is a poetic description of one simple truth: you should *love* God's plan for avoiding sexual immorality. And this love that you have for God's plan, it needs to be a full love. It should be like the love that you have for your sister (the father is assuming that you do have a sister and that you do love her) and like the love that you would have for your wife. That's how you should treat God's plan: **Love it! (**Fill in the blank at the beginning of this section with the appropriate word.)

But what does this mean on a practical level? **In the space below, describe some practical ways that you can love your sister, and describe the kind of love that you are supposed to have for your wife.**

_____

_____

_____

Isn't this an amazing image? Your love for God's plan should be deeply loyal, protective, and unconditional like your love for your sister. And like your love will be for a wife, so you should have a passionate, emotional, powerful, unconditional love for God's plan. In other words, you need to delight in God's plan like you will delight in your wife.

Fill in the blanks below to record all three steps that Proverbs 7:1–5 gives for how you should treat God's plan.

Step 1: T_____ it! (Proverbs 7:1–2)

Step 2: M_____ in it! (Proverbs 7:3)

Step 3: L_____ it! (Proverbs 7:4)

You are supposed to treat God's plan as the ultimate antidote for the foolishness of sexual immorality. You are being challenged to love God's Word; to see it as your closest friend, not as your enemy; to make a radical commitment to keep it close to you, around you, within you. This is how you should treat God's plan.

On Day One you learned that the most important issue in *Great Love* boils down to the simple choice: *Will you accept God's plan for avoiding sexual immorality?* So what about it? Are you getting closer to making your decision? Have you already made it? You've spent the last three days learning how God wants you to treat His plan. Are you beginning to realize that accepting God's plan for avoiding sexual immorality means that you will trust that His plan is *the* only real plan? Your own plans may have some wisdom in them, but His plan is the wisest plan, the best plan. Are you willing to commit to treasure this plan, to marinate your life in this plan, to passionately love it?

pray   Spend the next few minutes in prayer. Imagine Jesus Christ standing or sitting beside you. Talk honestly to Him about these things you are learning. **Read Proverbs 7:1–5 again, imagining in your mind that the Lord Christ is actually pleading with you, right now, right where you are to accept His plan.** What do you need to say to Him? Do you need to ask Him for courage or strength to obey? Do you simply need to thank Him for speaking to you? Do you need to hear His gracious offer of a second chance? Do you need to ask for the grace to forgive yourself and to receive His loving forgiveness as you make a fresh start? **Spend a few moments in real conversation over what you are hearing.**

Week Two: Day Four
What Is God's Plan? (Part 1)

Psalm 46:10 is often translated: "Be still and know that I am God." The word that is translated "be still" means to "relax" or "let go" or "refrain." It's a command (an imperative). In this verse God commands you to relax, to let go of all your activities for a moment, to slow down and be still. And here's the key: the reason He commands you to "be still" is because that is one of the fundamental ways you get to "know that He is God."

The moments of prayer at the beginning and end of each session in *Great Love* are designed to lead you on a journey of hearing God's voice deep in your innermost being. Sure, there are times when God speaks loudly, getting your attention immediately and completely. However, throughout the Bible God teaches you to grow into the kind of person who is constantly aware of His presence. To develop this kind of relationship with God you must learn to "be still" before Him. Too often we rush into God's presence and talk before we listen.

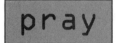

Pause for a moment. Quiet your mind and listen. Can you hear the whispers of His presence? Can you remember the last time that you felt His nearness, when you walked together and you let Christ embrace you in His love?

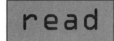

Take your time to read Proverbs 7:1–27, slowly. Allow yourself to dwell on anything that strikes you.

You've learned that deciding whether you will or will not accept God's plan for avoiding sexual immorality is the most important decision of *Great Love.* You've learned how God wants you to treat this plan for avoiding sexual immorality: treasure it, marinate in it, and love it. But you have yet to learn what that plan actually is. Today and tomorrow you will discover that it is actually very simple.

Part 1: G_____ your h_____! (Proverbs 7:24–25)

Read Proverbs 7:24–25.

When it comes to following God's plan for resisting sexual immorality, the biggest issue God wants to address is your heart. It is here where you win or lose the battle to remain sexually pure. The devil wants to destroy you in every way, and your heart is the main area he will attack in order to lead you down the destructive path of sexual immorality. **So what do you think it means in Proverbs 7:25 when you are told, "Do not let your heart turn aside to her ways" (NASB), or "Don't let your hearts stray away toward her" (NLT)? Use the space below to answer this question.**

_____

_____

_____

_____

_____

_____

Above all else, guard your heart, for it affects everything you do.
—Proverbs 4:23 (NLT)

The battle is fought in the heart. For your heart to go toward sexual immorality means that you have been persuaded that sexual immorality is something you want. You might continue to wear the True Love Waits ring, you may still be a virgin, you may not even have a girlfriend, but in your heart you find yourself thinking about sex a lot. You desire to see girls naked. You find yourself desiring to fool around. In other words, your desires, your mind, your imagination are going through the motions. This is an extremely important point: so many people think that they are okay because they are not physically engaging in intercourse outside of marriage. They don't realize that the first and most important battlefield is in their heart—their thoughts, feelings, desires, imagination, and will.

read

Read Proverbs 4:23 (it's in the margin of this page).

Guard your heart! Finally you've gotten here. Here you have it—the first part of God's plan for avoiding sexual immorality. Fill in the appropriate blanks at the beginning of this section, next to **Part 1.**

To effectively guard your heart, you need to be aware of the main ways that the devil will attack. These are the three doorways into your heart: your eyes, your ears, and your brain. **In the doorway below draw an image that represents your eyeballs.** (If you hate drawing, just write the word "eyes" in the doorway.)

I made a covenant with my eyes not to look with lust upon a young woman.
—Job 31:1 (NLT)

In the box under the doorway, record some of the things that you *see* that fuel the fires of lust in your life. For example: pornography, looking down a girl's shirt, looking up skirts, looking at magazines with sexual pictures in them, watching specific movies, etc.

Read Job 31:1 (it's in the margin) and then copy the verse onto the lines below the box.

In the doorway below, draw an image that represents an ear. (If you hate drawing, just write the word "ear" in the doorway.)

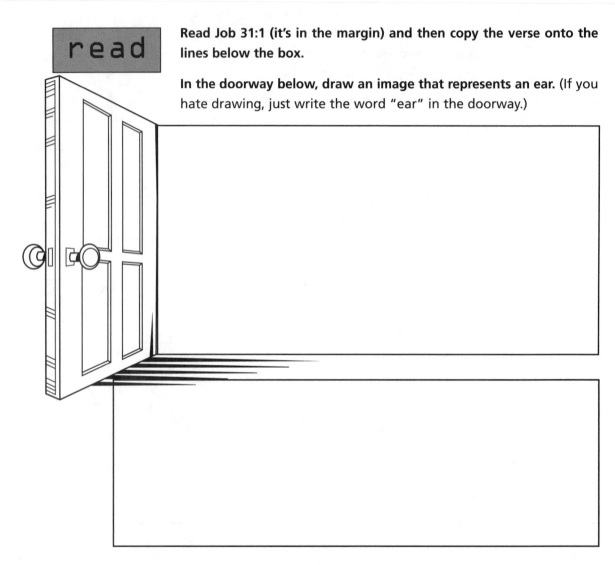

In the box under the doorway, record some of the places and ways that you *hear* things that fuel the fires of lust in your life. For example: talking and joking about things of a sexual nature, movies, music, locker room, lunch table, etc. You already learned (in the first week) that this is one of the steps down the path to sexual immorality. It is a crucial way that Satan creates in you a desire for sexual activity.

In the doorway below draw a brain. (If you hate drawing, just write the word "brain" in the doorway.)

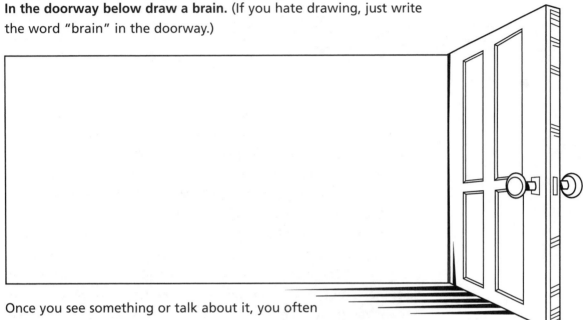

Once you see something or talk about it, you often begin to think about it over and over—this is called *meditation*. You *should* meditate—but on God's Word, not on lustful thoughts. Napoleon once said, "Imagination governs the world." Your imagination is a gift from God to be used for God and for His glory (remember the section on "marinate in God's plan"), but because it is so powerful, Satan wants to use it for powerfully evil purposes—like imagining sexual immorality. This is why it is so dangerous to look at, listen to, and talk about things that give your brain fuel for lust.

Think of your mind as a gas tank. In order to stop burning with lust you need to stop putting fuel in your tank. Guys have areas of weakness, areas that Satan uses frequently to tempt with lust. Think of these areas as the gasoline. If you want to stop burning with lust, you need to stop refueling. **In the space below, make a list of the six biggest things that fuel your lust. What are the areas, the experiences, the images, the conversations that give fuel to**

your lust-tank? Here are some examples: lingerie advertisements, female joggers in tight outfits, billboards showing scantily-clad women, beer-and-bikini commercials, movies rated PG-13 or higher, girls at school who dress sexually.

_____

_____

_____

_____

Guard your heart, that's the first part of God's plan. Notice that Proverbs 7:25 _first_ tells you to guard your heart, and _then_ says that you should not stray into her paths. So you don't simply avoid sexual immorality by deciding to stay off the path to her house. You avoid the path by guarding your heart. Nearly every time a person goes down the path of sexual immorality, it is because they have already lost the battle in their heart. God's plan is for you to avoid the path to sexual immorality by first of all guarding your heart against Satan's fuel for lust. God is calling you to declare war on the internal battle-field, the battlefield that no one else can see. God is asking you to get serious about guarding your heart. Proverbs 4:23 says this very bluntly: "Above all else, guard your heart, for it affects everything you do." (NLT).

If you accept God's plan and declare war on Satan right now and you start the battle in your heart, what practical changes do you need to make? **Based on what you've learned (about the three doorways, etc.), use the space below to record specific actions you need to take.**

_____

_____

_____

_____

Imagine that Jesus is standing or sitting beside you. Talk to Him about what you have just written. Talk just like you are sharing this with your closest friend. **Open your heart up to Christ, and talk about what He's doing in your life through** *Great Love.*

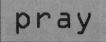

Week Two: Day Five

What Is God's Plan? (Part 2)

Saint Ignatius once wrote, "In these days, God taught me as a school-teacher teaches a pupil." Can you say this of the last few weeks? Has God been teaching you as you've spent time studying, meditating on, and praying with His Word? Remind yourself that God has more to teach you. **Ask God for the grace to hear His voice and to let Him form you into His image.**

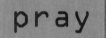

Read Proverbs 7:1–27. Listen carefully for the gentle promptings of the Holy Spirit to slow down and meditate, to pray, to respond, to act.

Part 2: G_____ the h_____! (Proverbs 7:22–23, 26–27)

Read Proverbs 7:22–23, 26–27. What is the father saying about the result of sexual immorality?

_____

_____

_____

_____

_____

_____

"Stolen water is sweet; and bread eaten in secret is pleasant." But he does not know that the dead are there, that her guests are in the depths of Sheol.
—Proverbs 9:17–18

The father is saying to the son, "Remind yourself of one thing: when you walk into the bedroom of sexual immorality, look around the bed and you will see the bones of dead men. The passion of this sex is sweet, but it is also a deadly poison. Sexual immorality is like a black widow; after the ecstasy of the moment, it will eat you alive!"

You must believe that this is reality. Let it scare the death out of you. Know that this will be your fate. And you won't be the first or the last: sexual immorality is a mass murderer. When you ignore God's commands and allow your hormones to be your god, then you will be burned.

Stop here for a minute. Back up and think about this. Is sin fun? Seriously, be honest. Do you think that sexual activity outside of marriage (whether you are going all the way, fooling around, or just lusting) can be fun?

❏ **Yes**   ❏ **No**

The Bible gives an answer to this question. **Check out Proverbs 9:17–18** (it's in the margin).

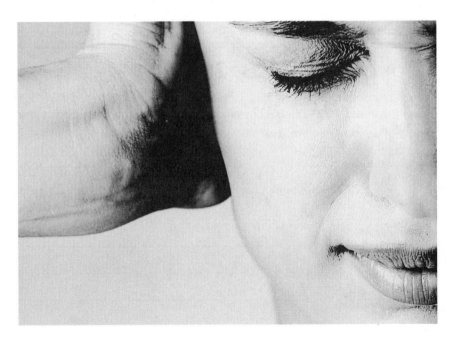

Great Love for Guys

This poetic passage openly admits to the "sweetness" of "stolen water," which in Proverbs 9:17–18 clearly means adultery. So the Bible is telling you that sexual immorality can be fun. Proverbs 9:17 is a blatantly honest passage of Scripture about the pleasures of sin. Sex outside of marriage can be sheer ecstasy. But there is more. The very next verse (Proverbs 9:18) tells you to be aware that you will get more than pleasure out of sexual immorality. "But he does not know that the dead are there, that her guests are in the depths of Sheol" (Proverbs 9:18). Look at Proverbs 6:27–28 (it's in the margin). This passage gives a very effective visual image. On a literal level, it is frightening. If someone put a burning piece of wood in their lap, surely they would be burned. But in the surrounding context of these two verses (Proverbs 6:20–35) you clearly see that the subject being discussed in such a powerfully poetic way is actually sexual immorality. This passage is a picture of the danger of sexual immorality.

Can a man scoop fire into his lap and not be burned? Can he walk on hot coals and not blister his feet?
—Proverbs 6:27–28 (NLT)

So, to be completely honest, sexual immorality can be fun, but it will burn you. That's why the final step in God's plan for avoiding the path to sex outside of marriage is: **Grasp the hurt.** Fill in the appropriate blanks at the beginning of this section.

Proverbs 7:22–23, 26–27 gives many different images (some people identify up to eight different images) of the result of traveling the path to sexual immorality. **In the space provided, list these images.**

read

_____

_____

_____

_____

_____

_____

_____

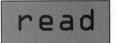 **Read through Proverbs 7:22–23, 26–27 one more time and this time go slow. Pay attention to these images. Imagine them in your mind as if they are being played out on a movie screen.**

Which images impact you the most powerfully? In the space below, sketch a quick picture of these.

What does it mean to *grasp the hurt?* It means that you are to let these images burn their way into your mind, into your heart, into your soul; that you are to believe, embrace, and be persuaded by this teaching on sexual immorality. The reason that the father piled up graphic image on top of graphic image is so that you will never forget the awful destruction caused by sexual immorality.

Let's review. **Fill in the appropriate words to remind yourself of the six steps that lead down the path of sexual immorality.** (You learned about these last week.)

Six Steps to Sexual Immorality
1.

2.

3.

4.

5.

6.

Do you remember what you marked last week as steps that you are already taking and need to repent of? Are there any marks that you need to add? Has God revealed to you some new areas that you weren't ready to be honest about last time, or areas that you didn't even realize were a part of your life? **If so, mark those now.**

Yesterday and today you learned the specific contents of God's plan for avoiding sexual immorality. **Fill in the blanks below with the names of the two parts to this plan.**

1.

2.

Earlier this week you learned how God wants you to treat His plan. **List the three ways below.**

1.

2.

3.

Each day you were instructed to read through the entire chapter (Proverbs 7). One of the reasons is so that you would begin to notice the big picture and not just the individual verses. In fact, when you look at the overall chapter, you see that the real issue is the choice you were presented with on Day One. **Remember, this is the most important decision that you will face in *Great Love*! Will you trust God enough to accept His plan for avoiding sexual immorality?** On Day One you read that this was the challenge of Proverbs 7:1–5. However, it is not just the challenge of Proverbs 7:1–5 but of the entire chapter. In fact, this challenge is kind of like a set of bookends on a bookshelf—it holds Proverbs 7 together. It's like a frame on a picture; it surrounds everything within the chapter. It literally wraps around the entire passage. **Look closely at the beginning of the chapter. Look at Proverbs 7:2.**

read

*Keep my commands
and live.*
—Proverbs 7:2

*Her house is the way to
Sheol, descending to the
chambers of death.*
—Proverbs 7:27

Now look at the end of the chapter, at Proverbs 7:27.

Do you see the deliberate contrast? In the beginning the father tells his son to choose God's plan in order to *live*. At the end, the father tells the son that if he chooses the immoral path, he will *die*. By framing the chapter with this focused message, the father wants you to know that this is the main idea of the chapter. **In the space below, draw two images: one to represent "life" (Proverbs 7:2) and one to represent death (Proverbs 7:27).**

So what is it? What's the verdict? What will you choose?
Will I accept God's plan for avoiding sexual immorality?

❏ Yes   ❏ No

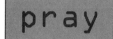

In the final moments of today's session, talk with God about your decision, about what you have learned, about what you sense God is saying to you. Honestly share joy and fear, confusion and confidence, excitement and dread. Remember, Jesus is there with you, sitting in front of you.

There is a very old and very common prayer that Christians throughout the world have prayed. It's called "The Doxology." As you finish your time today, recite this to the Lord:

*Glory be to the Father,
and to the Son,
and to the Holy Spirit;
as it was in the beginning,
is now, and ever shall be,
world without end. Amen.*

God's Plan for Great Dating

Introduction

Great Love. That's what God has for you, and that's the type of love God wants you to experience. God desires nothing but the very best for you, and coming from God that is something to get excited about. His plans for you are so good, so pleasurable that you cannot even imagine them. You would blow a circuit before you ever fully grasped the immense beauty, the astonishing goodness, and the intoxicating delight of God's designs for you.

This does not mean that Christianity is always easy. In fact, sometimes it's very painful. After all, at the center of the Christian faith is the brutal, bloody, and gruesome crucifixion of Jesus Christ. The cross wasn't pretty, and it certainly wasn't easy—not for Jesus and not for His followers (which includes you). You see, when Jesus explained to His followers what it meant to be a Christian, He told them: "If anyone wishes to come after Me, he must deny himself, and take up his cross and follow Me. For whoever wishes to save his life will lose it; but whoever loses his life for My sake will find it" (Matthew 16:24–25).

To follow Jesus you must deny yourself and take up your cross. Think about what this means for your dating life. To follow Jesus when it comes to dating, you must deny yourself and even die to some of your "rights." According to the world, you have a "right" to date whomever you want to date. You have a "right" to kiss and fool around. However, as a Christian your first commitment is to follow Jesus. And following Jesus may mean that you have desires and rights that need to be surrendered.

At the center of Christianity is the death of Christ on the cross. If you want to date in such a way that pleases God, then at the center of your dating life must be the death of your own plans on your own cross. But remember, the cross is not the end of the story. Jesus rose from the dead, in victory over death and evil. In the same way, when you die to your own plans for dating, God will resurrect your dating life in His great love. That's the ironic thing: "For whoever wishes to save his life will lose it; but whoever loses his life for My sake will find it" (Matthew 16:25). If you die to your own plans for dating, you will find real excitement, joy, satisfaction, and pleasure in your dating life. Bottom line: God's way works!

Get ready! You are about to go on the wild journey of discovering God's plan for your dating life. Along the way, you will discover some ideas and desires that you have which you need to take to the cross with you. Just remember, you can't out-give God. God's great love for you will replace whatever you surrender with something beyond your wildest dreams!

Week Three: Day One
Biblical Priorities for Dating (Part 1)

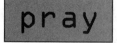

Remember Psalm 46:10— "Be still [relax, let go, refrain] and know that I am God." Take a few moments to do what God instructs in this verse. Relax your body. Relax your mind. Realize that Jesus Christ is already here. He was here before you arrived, waiting patiently because He loves to spend time with you. **Greet Him, thank Him for His presence, ask Him for guidance as you study His Word.**

To honor God in your dating life, it is essential to establish the right priorities. Today and tomorrow you will explore four fundamental priorities for dating in a way that pleases God.

Priority 1:
S_____ to G_____ p_____

Read Genesis 3:1–6.

In verses 4–5 you find the basis of almost every temptation. The serpent tells Eve, "You won't die!...God knows that your eyes will be opened when you eat it. You will become just like God, knowing everything, both good and evil" (NLT). The serpent was tempting Eve by trying to get her to doubt God's motives. He was saying, "Hey Eve. That fruit that God told you to stay away from—yeah, that nice, plump, juicy fruit. You see it, don't you? Looks good, doesn't it? And it is good. It's real good. In fact, that's why God doesn't want you to eat it. God told you to stay away from it because He knows that if you eat it, you will be blessed. You see, Eve, God doesn't want you to have the blessing of that fruit. God is holding back on you."

Now look really close at verse 6. (It's in the margin.) This verse says that Eve "saw" three things about the fruit and the tree. **What three things did she "see"?**

read

When the woman saw that the tree was good for food, and that it was a delight to the eyes, and that the tree was desirable to make one wise, she took from its fruit and ate; and she gave also to her husband with her, and he ate.
—Genesis 3:6

read

_____

_____

_____

After talking with the serpent, Eve looked at the fruit and said, "Hey. That does look really good. It looks like it would taste great, and it will make me wise." Upon speaking with the serpent, then, Eve saw the fruit in a *different* way than she had seen it before. She saw it as *something good that God was withholding from her.*

From the rest of the story (Genesis 3—Revelation 22), you know that the serpent was lying—that when Adam and Eve ate the fruit they didn't get something good, they lost something good. They lost the garden, they lost their intimate relationship with God, they lost their

innocence—they lost so much. You see, the real temptation is this: *Do you trust God when He gives you His plans or do you trust in your own logic and desires?*

_____

_____

_____

_____

That is the bottom line of everything *Great Love* teaches on sexual purity. You must decide if you will trust God enough to trust His plan for your sexuality, for your dating life, and for all of life. Do you really believe that God has your best interests in mind? Or to put it another way, do you really believe that God is good?

This is the same challenge that you faced last week. It's a challenge that you will come back to throughout *Great Love*. If you want to be pure and holy, to please God with your life, then you must commit to accept God's plan for your life. You must choose to discover God's will and to trust Him enough to follow it—even when you don't understand it, even if you don't like it, and even if you disagree with it. This week you will be faced with the same basic question that you dealt with last week. It's okay that you are coming back to this, though. In fact, you will find that throughout your Christian life, this issue continues to come up again and again. It is one of those things that you are supposed to deal with over and over. It is central to what Christianity is all about. "Do you really believe that God is good? Will you trust God enough to accept His plan?" And this week, you will face this in the specific context of dating. "Do you believe that God's plan for your dating life is *good*? Will you trust God enough to accept His plan for your dating life?"

Eve ate the fruit because she doubted that God really had her best interests in mind. She doubted God's goodness. She believed instead that God was holding back something from her that was really good for her. What about you? **In what ways have you**

doubted God's goodness? Is there anything that you are doing now because you believe it is good or fun, even though God has told you to do otherwise?

_____

_____

_____

God is trustworthy. The One who created you loves you. Your creator became a human and died a cruel death on a cross in order to bless you (John 3:16). It is crazy to think that God would go to such extravagant lengths for you (becoming a human and dying on the cross) if He didn't want to bless you in every way. That's why John 10:10 says, "The thief's purpose is to steal and kill and destroy. My purpose is to give life in all its fullness" (NLT). If you want to honor God in your dating life, you must start here. **Surrender to God's plan**—this must become your number one priority in dating. Fill in the blanks at the beginning of this section next to **Priority 1**.

Pause for a moment. Picture Jesus Christ sitting or standing across from you. As honestly as you can, commit to trust Him when it comes to His plan for your dating life. Ask Him to show you the areas in your life where you have been tricked by the devil into believing that God is holding back something good from you. Ask Him to teach you what it means to trust Him in the details of your dating life. **Then listen closely and use the space below to record anything that you think He may be saying to you or showing you.**

`pray`

So the first priority is to **Surrender to God's plan** for your dating life. It's time to move on to the second basic, foundational priority that you must make if you want to pursue holiness and integrity while dating.

Priority 2:
L_____ f_____ to G____ for s_____

There's a guy in the Bible by the name of Asaph. He's not very well known, but this guy was a stud for God. Don't misunderstand; he didn't always have a radical trust in God. In fact, if you take the time to read through Psalm 73, you will see that he starts out really struggling in his relationship with God. He was full of envy and jealousy when he saw that people who did not live life according to God's plan seemed to be having a great time (Psalm 73:2–3). These people were prosperous (verse 3), and they didn't seem to ever get sick (verse 4) or be in trouble (verse 5). Surely they should have had a hard life; after all, they were bad people, full of pride and violence (verse 6). They had no self-control in their thought life (verse 7). Not only were they were wicked and mean (verse 8), they liked to make fun of God (verse 9)!

It was a beautiful letdown, the day I knew that all the riches this world had to offer me would never do.
—from "Beautiful Letdown" by Switchfoot

From Asaph's perspective, God didn't seem to care—He didn't try to stop them. In fact, He seemed to bless them instead of punish them (verses 10–12). When Asaph saw how the wicked and evil people were getting along just fine without God, he thought to himself, "My life has been a waste—wasted on living according to God's plan. I should be the one who is prospering, enjoying good health, and relaxing in the good life, but instead I've got nothing but pain and trouble. My life is one big problem and disappointment. It's not fair. I've tried to honor God; surely I should be blessed like the wicked people are blessed, and they should be suffering like I'm suffering" (see verses 13–14.)

From the rest of this psalm you learn that the problem was that Asaph was not satisfied with God alone. He wanted God *and* the good life. He wanted to have God *and* to have lots of money. He wanted to have a good relationship with God *and* to be popular. He wanted more than God; He wanted God *and* lots of cool stuff. Why did Asaph want this stuff? Because he thought it would satisfy him.

But then something happened: Asaph went to the temple (verses 16–17). There Asaph encountered God, and he realized that having God in his life was actually everything his soul really wanted. He realized that all that stuff (money, popularity, awards, etc.) couldn't really satisfy the hole in his soul. He realized what Ecclesiastes teaches, that only God can satisfy.

Great Love for Guys

With Asaph you discover the second priority that is absolutely crucial for a dating life that pleases God. You must recognize, accept, and embrace the fact that only God can satisfy you, that God made you with a piece of eternity in your soul (Ecclesiastes 3:11), and that piece of eternity causes you to hunger and thirst for significance and love. Your appetite for this is so large, as large as eternity, that only God can fill it. No girl, no accomplishment, absolutely nothing but God can satisfy you, because God made you to be satisfied with Himself alone. All that other stuff is nice. It's something to be enjoyed—but don't ever think it can really satisfy your soul.

He has also set eternity in their heart.
—Ecclesiastes 3:11

You are not prepared to date until you get to the point where you can genuinely and honestly say that you are not expecting a girl to satisfy you. Why? Because you will expect that girl to give you something that she can't possibly give you—satisfaction! Only God can satisfy your soul. And that's the second priority. **Look first to God for satisfaction.** Fill in the blanks at the beginning of this section next to **Priority 2**.

Remember this: jealousy and envy are good signs that you are looking for something other than God to satisfy your soul. What or who are you jealous of? Someone who is a better athlete? Who has a better home life? Better clothes? A better physique? Someone who is smarter? More popular? More talented? **Use the space below to record any jealousies or envies that you may have. Then, in a time of prayer, share these with God and ask Him for deliverance from the bondage of jealousy. Ask Him to help you, like Asaph, to stop looking for other things to satisfy and to realize that He alone can satisfy your soul.**

_____

_____

_____

_____

_____

Once again, picture Jesus Christ sitting or standing next to you. Spend the next few moments listening for His voice. If Jesus were trying to tell you something, would you know? If Jesus were challenging you, or encouraging you, would you hear His voice? Ask Him for the grace to receive what He is trying to say to you. **Listen and have a conversation with Him.**

Week Three: Day Two
Biblical Priorities for Dating (Part 2)

Just like yesterday, remember Psalm 46:10— "Be still [relax, let go, refrain] and know that I am God." Spend a few minutes doing this. Relax. Close your eyes and take a deep breath. Remind yourself that Jesus Christ is already here. He was here before you arrived, waiting patiently to spend this time with you. **Greet Him. Thank Him for His presence. Ask Him for guidance as you study His Word.**

Beginning tomorrow, you will explore practical guidelines from the Bible that will help you know more specifically *how* to date. Before getting there, though, you will spend today focusing on two final priorities that you must establish up front if you want to glorify God through your dating life. These two priorities deal with the kind of girl that a Christian guy should date.

Priority 3:
O_____ d_____ a C_____ g_____

Read 2 Corinthians 6:14–7:1.

Read verse 14 again.

While this passage of Scripture applies to several different areas of your life, the main thing that Paul (the person who wrote this part of the Bible) is addressing is marriage between a Christian and a non-Christian. Simply put, a Christian is not supposed to marry a non-Christian. **Look closely through the passage again, and use the space below to record the reason that you think Paul gives for telling Christians to only marry other Christians.**

_____

_____

_____

_____

_____

_____

_____

No Missionary Dating

Too often guys decide that they can win their girlfriend to the Lord. Sometimes they try to defend what they are doing by arguing that even though she is not a Christian, the girl is very moral and nice.

It is definitely true that there are some people who are not Christian and yet are caring, giving, and morally impressive. However, the Bible is clear on this issue—Christians must not be in an intimate relationship with someone who is not a Christian. You should be friends with unbelievers (1 Corinthians 5:9–13) and through your friendship show them the love, joy, and peace that you find in Christ. Ask God to use you to lead them to Christianity, but do not cross the line and enter into a dating relationship with a non-Christian. Only when she becomes a Christian should you even consider dating her.

In some ways this passage in 2 Corinthians is a difficult passage. But basically Paul is saying that to enter into an intimate relationship with someone who is not a Christian is to initiate a relationship in which there is a fundamental incompatibility. This is what "unequally yoked" means.

⁹When I wrote to you before, I told you not to associate with people who indulge in sexual sin. ¹⁰But I wasn't talking about unbelievers who indulge in sexual sin, or who are greedy or are swindlers or idol worshipers. You would have to leave this world to avoid people like that. ¹¹What I meant was that you are not to associate with anyone who claims to be a Christian yet indulges in sexual sin, or is greedy, or worships idols, or is abusive, or a drunkard, or a swindler. Don't even eat with such people.
—1 Corinthians 5:9–11 (NLT)

Obviously, to be married to someone is very different than to be dating someone. In our culture, dating is often treated as something that is not all that serious. That's why some guys just jump from girlfriend to girlfriend. However, as a Christian you will begin to realize that dating is actually a very serious thing, something that you should treat with the utmost respect. Therefore, when the Bible reveals a principle for marriage such as "only marry a Christian girl," then you should recognize a principle that will help you to date in a way that pleases God.

Think about it: to be unequally yoked in a dating relationship means that you are in effect dating someone who does not believe that Christ is crucial to a healthy relationship. Furthermore, if you fall in love, sooner or later you will have to compromise, or break up, or marry. If you do get married then you are in for a lifetime (unless she becomes a Christian) of pain as you cannot share the most significant part of your life—your relationship with Christ—with the most significant person in your life. This goes against so much of what the Bible teaches. Based upon 2 Corinthians 6:14–7:1, and many other passages in the Bible, it is clear: a Christian guy should **Only date a Christian girl.** Fill in the blanks at the beginning of this section with the appropriate words next to **Priority 3**.

Priority 4:
O_____ d_____ a s_____
C_____ g_____

read **Read 1 Corinthians 5:9–13.** (It's in the margin.) In these verses you will discover one more critical priority for a guy who wants to date in a way that pleases God.

read Paul (the person who wrote this portion of Scripture) is telling the Christians who live in the city of Corinth that they should have a *double standard* when it comes to people who are immoral. **Read through the passage again and use the space below to record the different**

Great Love for Guys

ways that you should treat a person who is immoral, depending on if they are a Christian or a non-Christian.

_____

_____

_____

_____

_____

If someone claims to be a Christian but they are living a life full of sin (whether it is sexual sin, greed, idol worship, violence, drunkenness, stealing, etc.) then don't associate with that person—don't even eat with them. However, if the person _does not_ claim to be a Christian—if the person who is full of sin doesn't even profess faith in Christ—then you _should_ associate with him or her.

For many people today, this may sound weird, new, or radical. But make no mistake about it: this is a biblical truth (Paul also wrote about it in 2 Thessalonians 3:6, 14–15 and Titus 3:10.) Furthermore, Paul isn't the only biblical writer to discuss this. In fact, Jesus Himself teaches this same double standard. Check it out in Matthew 18:19–20.

Obviously, this brings up many issues, but for the purposes of _Great Love_ you should see how this applies to dating. **Once again, look at 1 Corinthians 5:11.**

When you apply this principle to your dating life it becomes clear that God wants you to demand much more from a girl than that she merely claims to be a Christian. In this verse you see a principle for dating that teaches you to **Only date a sold-out Christian girl.** Set your standards high. Only date a girl if she is radically committed to Christ. (Fill in the blanks at the beginning of this section next to **Priority 4**.)

The bottom line is pretty simple: if a girl claims to be a Christian but is living a hypocritical lifestyle, you should not be spending time with her, much less dating her.

You will also find this "double standard" in Matthew 18:15–20; 2 Thessalonians 3:6, 14–15; and Titus 3:10. As you think about this, it is important to realize that you need God's wisdom regarding timing. Also, everything must be in the context of committed Christian love. Finally, to successfully form friendships with a non-Christian who is living a life of blatant sin you must be deeply involved with a Christian group of friends. This will provide you with the necessary support structure to resist temptation.

read

Caution!

It is very important to notice both the cause and the purpose of the drastic step to "not associate with such a person" and "not even eat with such people." The cause is a sin that is intentionally and willfully *persisted* in. Paul is not referring to someone "messing up" accidentally. He is referring to someone who is living in sin to such an extent that it characterizes his or her life. Similarly, you learn from Titus 3:10 and Matthew 18:15–20 that this drastic step (where you no longer associate with the person or eat with them) should only occur after the person has been confronted in love and called to repentance. The purpose is to lead the sinning person to repentance and forgiveness (see 1 Timothy 1:20; 1 Corinthians 5:5; and Matthew 18:15–20).

So far this week you have been given a lot to read and think about. These four priorities that you are being challenged to establish in your life (in order to be prepared for dating in a way that pleases God) are tough. They require a lot from you. They demand a firm commitment to trust in the goodness of God's plan—even when you don't understand it fully, even when you don't like it very much, and even when you may disagree with it. In the space below, write out the four priorities. As you do, think carefully and prayerfully about each one. **Use the extra space below each to record any specific thing you think the Lord has revealed to you about your life through that particular priority.** (It may involve questions you have, changes you need to make, or ideas for remaining faithful. Be creative and listen close for God's voice.)

Priority 1:

Priority 2:

Priority 3:

Priority 4:

Expectations for a Wife

Now is the time for you to put all that you've learned to work in a very practical way. **In the space below, record a list of qualities that you should expect in your future wife.** Don't rush through this exercise. Take your time. In preparation, read Galatians 5:22–23 and 1 Corinthians 13:4–9. The passage in Galatians is often referred to as "The Fruit of the Spirit." These are qualities that develop in your life when you let God grow strong within you. The passage in 1 Corinthians is often referred to as "The Love Chapter." This is a beautiful description of what real Christian love looks like. You may want to begin your list with these qualities (both "The Fruit of the Spirit" and "The Love Chapter"). Also, review the four priorities for a Christian dater. Be sure to incorporate them into your list.

"My future wife will be..."

_____

_____

_____

_____

_____

_____

_____

_____

_____

Already Dating?

Perhaps you are already in a dating relationship. In light of what you are learning in this study, you may need to ask yourself some hard questions. For example, below is a great test for you to take to evaluate your current dating relationship.

The Dating Test

❑ Yes ❑ No   Are you more holy than you were when you began dating this person?

❑ Yes ❑ No   Are you closer to God than you were when you began dating this person?

❑ Yes ❑ No   Do you pray more?

❑ Yes ❑ No   Are you more passionate for worship?

❑ Yes ❑ No   Are you more involved in your youth group?

❑ Yes ❑ No   Are you more plugged in to the life of your church?

❑ Yes ❑ No   Are you more involved in serving through a ministry?

❑ Yes ❑ No   Do you read your Bible more?

❑ Yes ❑ No   Are your feelings and emotions dictated by your girlfriend? Do they revolve around the mood and opinions of your girlfriend? If so, get out.

❑ Yes ❑ No   Does the girl that you are dating now fulfill the list of expectations that you recorded in the previous activity?

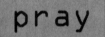

In these moments of prayer, you have lots of options. Perhaps you could conclude your prayer time by praying specifically for your future wife. There's really a lot of ways you can do this. Maybe you will pray through the list of expectations that you've developed. Praying that wherever she is right now, God will speak to your future wife and guide her into an intimate relationship with Himself so that she will become full of the fruit of the Spirit, and full of Christian love. Maybe you will pray for yourself, that you will patiently wait on the one God has planned for you. Maybe you will pray for the courage and the discipline necessary to only date a girl who fulfills your expectations. Or maybe you need to pray over a relationship that you are in at the moment. Maybe God is guiding you to make some changes in that relationship. Whatever you choose to pray about, carry on the practice that you have been establishing since you began *Great Love*. Imagine Jesus Christ sitting or standing in front of you. Remember that He is gazing on you with love. **Talk openly and honestly with Him about what you have been feeling and thinking as you studied His Word today.**

Week Three: Day Three
How to Date (Part 1)

God loves speaking to you, individually. Isn't that amazing? The God of this universe delights to talk specifically with you. Your job is to listen, to hear what He is saying to you. **Take a few moments to greet Jesus Christ and to share with Him your excitement about hearing Him speak to you today.**

Today you will switch gears. So far this week you've been learning about the priorities that should be established in your life in order to date in a way that pleases God. Now you'll begin to look more specifically and more practically at how to date. This involves three basic steps: (1) spend time alone with God every day, (2) establish relationships of accountability with some other guys, and (3) set boundaries for determining *how far is too far* when it comes to the physical aspect of your dating life. Today you will explore steps one and two. The remainder of the week will be devoted to the third step.

Step 1: G_____ a_____ w_____
G_____ e_____ d_____

Read 1 Peter 5:8.

read

This graphic and violent picture of Satan should help you realize what is at stake in the area of sexual temptation. In the verse, what picture is given to represent Satan? **Either write out a description in your own words or draw the image.**

read   In John 10:10 Jesus uses a different image to describe Satan's plans for you. **Read the verse, then use the space below to draw the image that Jesus presents.** (If you aren't the artsy type, feel free to write a description in words.)

In 1 Peter 5:8, Satan is portrayed as a ravenous lion seeking to devour you. His only goal is your complete destruction. Jesus put it in a different way, describing Satan as a murderous robber: "The thief's purpose is to steal and kill and destroy" (John 10:10 NLT). In *Great Love* you have been learning that one of the primary ways Satan seeks to destroy you is through sexual temptation. In other words, you are in a battle. War has been declared. You didn't ask for it. You didn't volunteer. But that's too bad. Satan has declared war on you and is attacking you in this area.

Since you are not fighting a human enemy, since your adversary is the devil himself, it is absolutely necessary that you connect with God on a daily basis. Some people call this a *quiet time*. However, your time with God doesn't always need to be quiet. Sometimes it may be very loud as you sing or shout, cry and sob, or confess and accuse. Perhaps it would be better to call this time *TAWG:* **T**ime **A**lone **W**ith **G**od. Doesn't that just hit the nail on the head? Isn't that exactly what you need to do each day? Spend some time where it is just you and God so that He can grow you into a strong Christian who is able to resist Satan's vicious attack. Fill in the blanks at the beginning of this section next to **Step 1** with the appropriate words: **Get alone with God every day**.

There are two basic elements to a successful *TAWG:* prayer and Scripture. As you've been learning in the directed prayer times at the beginning and end of each day's session in *Great Love*, prayer involves more than your words. It demands listening and focusing on the presence of God. It calls on you to remember God's activity in your life. It's really about cultivating a relationship with Jesus Christ in which you are aware throughout the day of His nearness. In this way, your entire life becomes your prayer. Similarly, the Scripture aspect of a *TAWG* can be fulfilled in a multitude of ways. It can involve in-depth Bible study, or simply reading and listening to Scripture, or memorizing God's Word. The basic issue is that you root your time with God in His Word. Sure, God does speak in other ways (through sermons, songs, nature, people, etc.), but the primary way that God speaks is through His Word. When you are spending *time alone with God*, it's important to let Him speak to you, and therefore it's important to receive His Word. Now, the order doesn't matter. Some people start out in prayer. Others start out in the Word. Don't get hung up on any set pattern. Just remember the purpose: *get alone with God and hear from Him, and let Him hear from you*. One day your heart may be full of praise and song, so you begin by singing. On another day you may need to read several chapters of Scripture before you are provoked into prayer. The goal is an encounter with the Living God so that your soul can feast in His presence.

Here are three basic benefits of a daily *TAWG*.

1. Makes you spiritually strong

It is written, "Man shall not live on bread alone, but on every word that proceeds out of the mouth of God."
—Matthew 4:4

Jesus answered by quoting Deuteronomy: "It takes more than bread to stay alive. It takes a steady stream of words from God's mouth."
—Matthew 4:4 (*The Message*)

2. Keeps you pure

How can a young man keep his way pure? By keeping it according to Your word.
—Psalm 119:9

Study this Book of the Law continually. Meditate on it day and night so you may be sure to obey all that is written in it. Only then will you succeed.
—Joshua 1:8 (NLT)

3. Helps you win the battle

Put on all of God's armor so that you will be able to stand firm against all strategies and tricks of the Devil. For we are not fighting against people made of flesh and blood, but against the evil rulers and authorities of the unseen world, against those mighty powers of darkness who rule this world, and against wicked spirits in the heavenly realms. Use every piece of God's armor to resist the enemy in the time of evil, so that after the battle you will still be standing firm.... Pray at all times and on every occasion in the power of the Holy Spirit. Stay alert and be persistent in your prayers for all Christians everywhere. —Ephesians 6:11–13, 18 (NLT)

Please don't misunderstand. Spending time alone with God on a daily basis will not guarantee you victory in the area of sexual purity. In fact, if you don't also take the next step you will almost certainly be another casualty for Satan to brag about.

Step 2: B_____ a_____

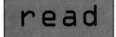

Read the following passages of Scripture: Proverbs 27:17 and Ecclesiastes 4:9–12.

These two passages present the advantages of having a friend to help you through life. **Use the space below to list some of these benefits.**

_____

_____

_____

_____

_____

Satan knows these passages of Scripture. He knows the profit of having someone to help you in your areas of weakness. He knows that you are a much easier target when you are alone. As a result, he will attempt to pull you away from close, godly friends when you begin to date. One of the simplest ways that Satan achieves this is through the very nature of having a girlfriend: you begin to spend so much time with her that you lose touch with other friends.

One of Satan's first attacks will often be an attempt to bring privacy and secrecy into your life. Sexual sin flourishes in the dark. Satan wants you to be unaccountable and alone. But don't let him get away with this. Fight him! Make this your battle line! *Refuse to be unaccountable*. Refuse to try to fight Satan by yourself. How? Simple! Find some godly guys with whom you can be honest about your struggles, weaknesses, failures, mess-ups, and victories. One of the best ways to frustrate Satan is to *refuse to let secrecy surround your behavior.*

Here's your challenge: Identify one, two, or three godly and righteous guys with whom you can be completely honest—guys who will keep your struggles and your weaknesses private, guys who will not humiliate you, but will guard your shame and help you work through your struggles before the Lord Christ. Some people call these people their accountability partners. **Record in the space below the names of some guys that can fulfill this role in your life.** (If you cannot think of anyone at this moment, then perhaps you need to take a day or two to pray about it and ask God to show you someone who would be a good accountability partner.)

For some, accountability is the hardest part of surrendering to God's plan for sexual purity. In fact, this is one of the fundamental mistakes in the American dating scene. The biblical principle of accountability teaches that if you are drifting away from your friends, then you are dating in a way that is consistent with the world's values, but it is entirely inconsistent with God's plan. Once again, the choice you face is whether you will accept God's wisdom on how to resist sexual immorality or not.

_____

_____

_____

_____

_____

_____

_____

Today you have a homework assignment. If you have thought of some potential accountability partners, then talk to them about this. Ask them if they will meet with you (either in person, on the phone, or online) on a regular basis (perhaps once each week). During your weekly meeting you must ask each other the hard questions and spend time in prayer. And you must confront one another, in love, when you sense that the other person is drifting from God or involved in a relationship that is out of God's will. The Bible is crystal clear about sexual sin: "But among you there must not be even a hint of sexual immorality, or of any kind of impurity" (Ephesians 5:3 NIV).

So you've got to be gentle but tough with each other. Here is a list of questions that you can ask one another in your meetings. **Feel free to add to, take away, or completely change this list so that it fits your specific needs.**

• What victories have you had this week?

• Have you prayed daily?

• Have you read your Bible daily?

• Have you lusted? Looked at any pornography? Fooled around with a girl?

• What else?

• Have you just lied to me?

• How can I pray for you this week?

• _____

• _____

• _____

• _____

Be Accountable! That's the second practical step for dating in a way that pleases God. Fill in the blanks at the beginning of this section next to **Step 2**.

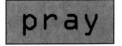

Throughout your time in *Great Love* today, Jesus Christ has been here with you. He's provoked your thoughts—gently nudging you, trying to direct you, trying to speak to you, trying to present Himself to you. Picture Him sitting or standing in front of you right now. Discuss what you have heard Him say. Be honest about your feelings and thoughts. **Talk with Him as one trusted friend to another.**

Week Three: Day Four
How to Date (Part 2)

Here is an amazing prayer that was written by a Christian in Kenya: "From the cowardice that dares not face new truth, from the laziness that is contented with half-truth, from the arrogance that thinks it knows all truth, Good Lord, deliver me." Did you get it? Do you need to slowly read it over a few more times, focusing on each word to really grasp the profound humility of this dangerous prayer?

Now imagine that Jesus is standing or sitting in front of you. Out of unconditional love He longs for you to abandon yourself into His hands so that He can form you by His grace. **Use the prayer from Kenya to speak to Christ at this time.**

pray

How far is too far? Great question, right? It's been asked a thousand times. Is it okay to kiss? Does God mind if I touch a girl's breast? What if we are just playing around and I give her a little pinch on the butt? What if we are fooling around but don't have sex, is that okay? What about oral sex? These are all important questions, and you will discover God's view on them as you continue your journey with *Great Love* today and tomorrow.

Remember, you have already discovered two practical steps to dating in a way that is holy and pleasing to God. Record those two steps below.

Step 1:

Step 2:

Today and tomorrow you will dig into the last step. Get ready—this is going to be one wild ride!

Step 3: Set your boundaries now

And a key boundary that you must decide on before you ever go on a date is: *How far is too far?* In the space below describe where you think the line is. **Give your answer to the question: *When it comes to the physical part of my relationship with a girl, how far is too far?*** Be specific. For instance, is touching a girl's breast too far? Kissing? Oral sex? Talking dirty? Tickling? Holding hands? What about simply being alone with a girl?

_____

_____

_____

_____

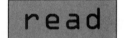

Let's see what Jesus says—after all, you've been constantly challenged to trust His plan for sexual purity. **Read Matthew 5:27–28.**

Based upon Jesus' words, where do you think the line is? How far is too far in Jesus' opinion? **Use the space below to record your answer.**

_____

_____

_____

_____

Did you notice that Jesus did not list any physical behaviors as "too far"? Look back at your answers to the previous question regarding what you thought was too far. Did you try to determine the line based upon physical actions? (To be fair, the examples given to help you get started were all physical actions, so maybe this influenced you to think along those lines.) The point is this: for Jesus the line is crossed when you begin to lust. That's right, the moment you lust you have gone too far. Based upon this passage of Scripture (and others like it), here is a Biblical definition of sexual immorality:

In God's eyes, sexual immorality is anything that I do for the purpose of sexual arousal, or anything that I continue doing once someone is sexually aroused.

Copy the definition into the space below.

_____

_____

_____

_____

_____

Jesus helps you to understand the answer to the question *How far is too far?* by presenting you with a godly view of sexual immorality: *anything that you do for the purpose of sexual arousal or anything that you continue doing once someone is sexually aroused.* By targeting lust, Jesus shows you that sexual immorality doesn't even always involve physical activities such as fooling around. **Use the space below to record some of the things that can cause you to become sexually aroused.** Make sure you include the things that don't even include physical touch. (If you are uncomfortable writing these things in your book, that's okay. You could write them on a separate sheet of paper, then tear it into tiny pieces and throw it away.)

_____

_____

_____

_____

_____

_____

To Kiss or Not to Kiss

Some Christians are completely against kissing before marriage. Other Christians have absolutely no problem with kissing. So what does the Bible say? It doesn't! So what should a person do? Well, that depends on a lot of factors. First of all, it depends on your parents. The Bible clearly teaches you to "obey your parents" (Ephesians 6:1). So if your parents don't want you kissing, it's an open and shut case. You need to honor your parents. What if your parents don't care? Well, you should consider your age. And remember, don't believe what the world tells you. You don't live by the same perspective as your surrounding culture. After all, you're a Christian, so you are seeking to please God, not conform to the world (Romans 12:1–2). Here are two more issues to consider when it comes to kissing: (1) Someone once said, "Kisses may not spread germs, but they certainly lower resistance." Kissing easily and often leads to other things. Why? Because that's the way God designed it. Somebody else once said, "Kissing power is stronger than will power." In other words, when you start kissing, it is often very difficult to resist temptation. (2) Kissing is the farthest you can go physically before you get married. So if you are doing this when you are 12 years old or 16 years old, then get ready for a long period of waiting. Until you get married, you can't go any further.

Another thing that you learn from this definition is that that sexual impurity can vary from one person to another, and from one moment to the next. That is, what might create arousal for one person may not for another. In addition, what may be sin for you at one moment may not be in another moment. Your sex drive is not a sin. It is normal for guys to have sexual thoughts pop up at unexpected times. These instantaneous thoughts are not sinful, but choosing to dwell on them is. Dwelling on them develops into arousal, and that becomes lust. For some people, brief kissing may be an appropriate way to share feelings, as long as it does not become so passionate that sexual arousal results. For other people, or the same person at another time, the slightest kiss does result in sexual arousal.

There are some behaviors that are definitely inappropriate at all times unless you are with your wife! Touching a girl's breasts, touching each other's genitals, stroking the top of the thigh, heavy kissing, kissing around the neck and chest, oral sex, and looking at one another naked are some of these. One of the most destructive lies that Satan uses to deceive many Christians is that you are not doing anything wrong if you are not having full-blown sex (intercourse). "After all, the Bible tells us not to have sex before marriage, and we aren't having sex. We're just fooling around." But this is not true. It's a lie straight from the pit of hell! The Bible does tell you not to have sexual intercourse before marriage, but it also tells you to avoid all *sexual activity* before marriage. (Remember what Jesus said in Matthew 5:27–28.) That is why it's so important to memorize and understand this definition of sexual immorality. **Use the space below to write out the definition of sexual immorality one more time. This time, try to write it from memory.** If you can't, then get a scrap of paper and write it over and over until you have it memorized.

_____

_____

_____

_____

_____

Based on this definition, is there anything going on in your life right now that is sexually immoral? Is there anything that you are deliberately doing even though you know that it will lead to arousal? Is there anything that you do, not intending to become aroused, but once you are aroused you continue anyway? Is there anything that you do in order to provoke arousal in someone else? Is there anything you do that causes someone else to be aroused, and you continue doing it anyway?

*I will forgive their wicked-
ness and will never again
remember their sins.*
—Jeremiah 31:34 (NLT)

*My blood…is poured out
to forgive the sins of
many.*
—Matthew 26:28 (NLT)

*There is forgiveness of sins
for all who turn to me.*
—Luke 24:47 (NLT)

*Now turn from your sins
and turn to God, so you
can be cleansed of your
sins.*
—Acts 3:19 (NLT)

*He [God] is so rich in
kindness that he pur-
chased our freedom
through the blood of his
Son, and our sins are forgiven.*
—Ephesians 1:7 (NLT)

Sin is an ugly fact of life. But it is something that you should nei-ther ignore nor make fun of. Instead, you should honestly face up to it. Did you know that Christianity is the only religion in the world that takes sin seriously and offers a satisfactory remedy for it? And the way that you enjoy this remedy is not by denying the disease, but by confessing the sin.

God offers you forgiveness through the death of Jesus Christ. God is a forgiving God. (See the verses in the margin.) However, to receive God's forgiveness for your sins you must confess them to God. This is clearly the case in 1 John 1:8–9 (NLT): "If we say we have no sin, we are only fooling ourselves and refusing to accept the truth. But if we confess our sins to him, he is faithful and just to forgive us and to cleanse us from every wrong." Did you notice the two times that the word "if" is used? Go back and circle them. These two "if" statements teach you that, if you say there is no sin in your life, you are deceiv-ing yourself; if you confess your sin, you receive forgiveness.

pray

Imagine that Jesus Christ is sitting or standing across from you. Can you see the nail scars on His hands and feet? Remember, His death was for you! He died for your salvation, and a significant part of that salvation involves the forgiveness of your sins. **Confess your sin to Him; be specific. Ask Him to forgive you.** Now receive His loving embrace as He forgives you completely!

Week Three: Day Five

How to Date (Part 3)

Remember that image from Saint Ignatius—the bland and shapeless tree trunk that could never believe that it could be sculpted into a beautiful statue? If it had the choice, it would certainly never submit to the chisel of the artist. Just like that artist can see what the tree trunk is *and* what the tree trunk can become, so God sees you. Your loving Creator sees what you are and He sees what you can become. Remind yourself of this. Close your eyes and imagine that Jesus is sitting or standing across from you, His heart overflowing with love for you. He sees not only who you are, He sees who you can be. He's been meeting with you every day as you go through *Great Love* because of His great love for you! **Ask Him for the grace to surrender to His work in your life.**

pray

In the space below, write the definition of sexual immorality that you memorized yesterday. (If you are still working on it, and do not have it completely memorized yet don't worry. Keep writing it over and over and you'll be able to commit it to memory.)

_____

_____

_____

_____

When some people ask, "How far is too far?" what they really want to know is, "How much physical involvement can I get away with before God is upset?" Sometimes, but not all of the time, this reveals that they are more interested in getting away with sexual behavior than they are in pleasing God. Instead of "How far is too far?" you should ask: "What will please God? What does it mean to be pure? What does purity look like in a dating relationship?"

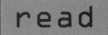

Read over the passages of Scripture listed below, then use the space provided to list some very practical and very specific changes that you need to make right now in order to fully obey what God instructs you to do in these verses.

Flee from youthful lusts and pursue righteousness, faith, love and peace, with those who call on the Lord from a pure heart.
—2 Timothy 2:22

_____

_____

Flee immorality. —1 Corinthians 6:18

_____

_____

Put on the Lord Jesus Christ, and make no provision for the flesh in regard to its lusts.
—Romans 13:14

_____

_____

But among you there must not be even a hint of sexual immorality, or of any kind of impurity.
—Ephesians 5:3 (NIV)

_____

_____

Are you beginning to realize that instead of seeing how close you can get to the edge without falling into sexual immorality, the Bible tells you to run away from the edge? You must be ruthless in eliminating every hint of sexual impurity from your life. Every hint. If you are holding hands and begin to be aroused—stop. If you are at a movie and something happens that arouses you—leave. Every hint. Be ruthless. If a girl is wearing something that arouses you…leave the area immediately. "Make no provision for the flesh in regard to its lusts" (Romans 13:14).

Obviously this is a very high standard. You live in a sex-saturated culture. Everywhere you look you see sex: TV, movies, music, billboards, books, magazines, the Internet. And then there are the conversations in the lunchroom, locker room, band hall, etc. The world is shouting out to you that sex is a normal part of being a teenager. But remember, God created sex as a wonderful gift to humans. As the creator, the inventor, the engineer of this gift, God knows how it works best. And God teaches you that sex is best only in marriage.

Too many Christians are living a double life. Their private life is consumed with lust and guilt, while their public life is spent pursuing God and leading others to know Christ. Too many Christians are trapped in this prison. Too many genuine Christians are struggling with the bondage of sexual immorality—going on mission trips in the summer, but fooling around with their girlfriend when they get home. Maybe you are highly involved in your youth group, but you still fantasize day and night about naked women. You can't sustain your focus on God during worship or prayer or Bible reading because of the guilt that consumes your soul. Every time something bad happens to you, you wonder if it is because of your sin. You have no peace. God seems distant. You feel alone. Falling in this area of sexual immorality is as easy as slipping off an icy log. You are sick of sinning. Sick of failing. Sick of Satan. Sick of yourself. You are tired of messing up. You have no courage in God's presence because you've failed Him so many times. You are humiliated by how many times you've asked forgiveness, only to mess up again. You are waiting and hoping and praying that God will take away your lustful desires. But God may not ever completely remove those desires. Instead, God promises the power to resist temptation. "His divine power has granted to us everything pertaining to life and godliness, through the true knowledge of Him who called us by His own glory and excellence" (2 Peter 1:3–4).

As obedient children, do not be conformed to the former lusts which were yours in your ignorance, but like the Holy One who called you, be holy yourselves also in all your behavior; because it is written, "You shall be holy, for I am holy."
—1 Peter 1:14–16

This is the will of God, your sanctification; that is, that you abstain from sexual immorality; that each of you know how to possess his own vessel in sanctification and honor, not in lustful passion, like the Gentiles who do not know God; and that no man transgress and defraud his brother in the matter because the Lord is the avenger in all these things, just as we also told you before and solemnly warned you. For God has not called us for the purpose of impurity, but in sanctification. So, he who rejects this is not rejecting man but the God who gives His Holy Spirit to you.
—1 Thessalonians 4:3–8

Therefore do not let sin reign in your mortal body that you should obey its lusts.
—Romans 6:12

But among you there must not be even a hint of sexual immorality, or of any kind of impurity.
—Ephesians 5:3 (NIV)

Marriage should be honored by all, and the marriage bed kept pure, for God will judge the adulterer and all the sexually immoral.
—Hebrews 13:4 (NIV)

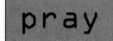**pray**

You've worked through *Great Love* Week Three: God's Plan for Great Dating. Where are you with God? Do you feel challenged or angry? Comforted or encouraged? Guilty or set free? Discouraged or thankful? **Open your heart up to Christ. Honestly talk with Him in response to how the Holy Spirit has been nudging you.** You may need to look over this week's material. Notice what you underlined, highlighted, and circled. Notice the prayers you wrote and the answers you gave.

What Does God Say About Homosexuality?

Introduction

Homosexuality has been around for thousands of years, and but it has never been as much a part of public life as it is today. You can probably name at least three television shows that have openly gay characters in them. What was once considered morally wrong is now considered in many communities to be a legitimate alternative lifestyle. For many teenagers, it has become so normalized that you no longer "feel" that it is bad or wrong. In fact, in many places homosexuality is becoming "cool."

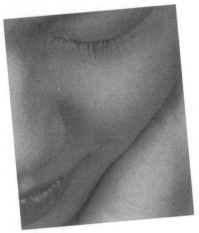

This most likely wasn't true for your parents, but you probably know someone who is openly gay, secretly gay, perhaps even a member of your family. You may be the issue yourself. The goal of this lesson is to help you learn the Biblical view of homosexuality, so that you can 1) learn to discern what is wrong with the world's view of homosexuality, 2) be equipped to minister to those who are struggling with homosexuality, and 3) be ministered to yourself if you are tempted by homosexuality.

The effects of homosexuality cover every aspect of life: physical, psychological, emotional, social, and spiritual. While we recognize the necessary role of this type of discussion, the concern of this study is to help you develop a Christian view of homosexuality. By exploring what the Bible says about homosexuality, you will see that the main issue for God is not the effects of homosexuality but the reason why homosexuality is wrong in the first place. You will learn that it is wrong because it violates God's intended plan for sex. From the very beginning of the Bible this plan insists that sex is to be enjoyed only between a man and a woman who are married to one another.

Because this is the way God created sex to be experienced, any experience of sex outside of a (heterosexual) marriage relationship is sinful. This is the reason that homosexuality is so destructive physically, psychologically, emotionally, socially, and spiritually.

There are three sessions (Day One through Day Three) on homosexuality: (1) What does the Old Testament Say About Homosexuality? (2) What does the New Testament Say About Homosexuality? (3) How Should Christians Treat a Person with Homosexual Desires? Day Four will explore the difference between temptation and sin, and Day Five will wrap up the Great Love study! So let's move forward together.

Week Four: Day One

What Does the Old Testament Say About Homosexuality?

As you begin, remember that Jesus Christ is here beside you. He's gazing upon you with love. **Take a moment to remind yourself of this, to thank God for His presence, and to thank Him for the time that you are about to spend together.**

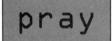

In the space below, list as many shows on TV or movies that you can think of which have a character identified as a homosexual or lesbian.

_____

_____

_____

_____

_____

_____

No doubt about it. Our society is saturated with the message that "Gay is okay." There seems to be an almost constant focus on homosexuality when you turn on the TV, go to the movies, or look at magazines. Teenagers have lots of different ways of responding to homosexuality—some treat it as funny and make crude jokes about it, some ignore it or respond as if it is normal, some became enraged and verbally abuse or even physically attack people who are struggling with homosexuality. Others think it's cool—the trendy thing in teenage making out. I want to challenge you to realize that this is a serious subject, and nothing to joke about. I also want to challenge you to realize that everyone who is struggling with homosexuality is a person, a person Jesus loves and died for. As a follower of Christ, we must view them with love and compassion.

Great Love does not refer to someone as "a homosexual." Instead, we will say "a person with homosexual attractions or desires," or "a guy who identifies himself as homosexual," etc. We believe that no person, especially a teenager, should be identified by their sexual feelings. Labeling someone only serves to reinforce a hurtful identity.

You might be struggling with homosexual feelings yourself. You may not know why—or maybe you do. Maybe you've been rejected by friends, classmates, neighbors, or parents so often that you feel like the word "loser" is tattooed on your forehead. Perhaps you have been abused, and you're filled with shame and despair. Some studies indicate that as many as 1 out of every 4 boys will be abused by the time they are 18 years of age. Maybe your father was missing from your life in some important ways. Maybe you aren't as athletic as other guys. Maybe you've never had any of these experiences, but you simply feel sexually attracted to other guys. Maybe your attraction to guys is unexplainable—it seems like a natural part of who you are. In fact, the vast majority of guys who have homosexual desires didn't ask for these feelings, and would have chosen to feel otherwise.

A Confession

I want to apologize for the way Christians so often respond in inappropriate ways to the issue of homosexuality. We often react in one of two extremes: (1) we use hateful, hurtful, abusive speech; we scream out with disgust, or (2) we ignore the subject, hoping that it will go away. When the church ignores homosexuality it can give someone the false impression that if they just pray hard enough then everything will turn out okay. When the Church is harsh and mean, it presents a false picture of Christ. For both of these reactions, Christians must repent. I'm sorry that the church has done such a poor job of loving you and helping you with your struggles.

What Is Homosexuality?

First of all, let's ask a very simple question. What exactly does the word *homosexual* mean? Webster's says, "1. Characterized by a tendency to direct sexual desire toward another of the same sex, and 2: relating to or involving sexual intercourse between persons of the same sex."

Before we go on, I need to point out one thing. It's not uncommon for teenagers to feel confused about their sexual identity. Because of this, the definition of homosexuality is properly only applied to adults. So if you are experiencing attractions to other guys, that doesn't necessarily mean that you are a homosexual. In fact, because homosexuality is so prominent in our culture, a disturbingly high percentage of teenagers have fleeting thoughts of attraction or arousal regarding members of the same gender. Research, however, indicates that the vast majority of these young people end up heterosexual.

Many people claim that "Gay is okay with God." Is this true? Today you will explore the main passages in the Old Testament that deal with homosexuality. (Tomorrow you will look at the main passages in the New Testament.)

Read Genesis 19:1–25. In the space below, briefly summarize (in two or three sentences) the passage in your own words.

read

_____

_____

_____

_____

_____

_____

One way to sum up this passage is to say that the men of Sodom attempted the violent homosexual rape of two angels, and God destroyed the city for its great wickedness.

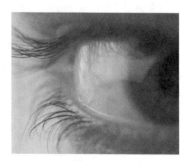

You learn from Genesis 18–19 that Sodom was wicked in many different ways; however, the prime example of their wickedness was this attempted homosexual gang rape. This event sealed the deal for God. He was convinced that the city deserved to be destroyed.

To be completely honest, the passage does not deal with a homosexual relationship between consenting adults. There are some people who argue that since Genesis 19 only highlights violent homosexual rape, then homosexual behavior is okay as long as no one is being forced into it. Let's see if the rest of the Bible can shed some light on this.

read

Read Leviticus 18:22.

How does God describe the sin of homosexual behavior in this passage?

_____

_____

_____

_____

_____

_____

_____

_____

_____

The Debate

Another popular interpretation by homosexual advocates is to claim that the sin of Sodom is the lack of social justice and hospitality. They usually point to the other Biblical passages that refer to this incident (Ezekiel 16:49–50; Jeremiah 23:14; 2 Peter 2:6; Jude 7). While it is true that some of these Biblical passages refer to Sodom's sin as the lack of social justice and hospitality, they do not dispute that homosexual rape was also a sin. Furthermore, Ezekiel 16:50 seems to indicate that homosexual rape was a significant part of God's reason for destroying the city.

Depending on the version of the Bible that you are reading, you should have written something like *abomination* or *detestable*. **Now read Leviticus 20:13.**

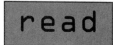

In this passage, what penalty is given for the sin of homosexual behavior?

_____

_____

_____

_____

_____

Homosexual behavior was one of the sins punishable by death in the Old Testament. Furthermore, in labeling it an "abomination" (or "detestable," or whatever word your translation of the Bible uses), God singles it out as especially bad. If you read surrounding verses, you will see that sexual sins such as adultery and incest were also punishable by death, as was cursing your mother or father.

It is true that Christians are not required to follow many of the laws in the Book of Leviticus. For example, we do not execute people who are caught in sexual sins. However, does this mean that the sin should be considered permissible? Let's see what the rest of the Bible has to say about it. Tomorrow you will explore the two key passages regarding homosexuality in the New Testament.

Spend the next few minutes asking God to cultivate in you His perspective on homosexuality. Ask Him to give you a true sadness for the sin. Ask Him to fill your heart with compassion and kindness for those who are struggling with this issue. If you are struggling with homosexual desires or habits yourself, spend this time talking with God about your feelings in response to today's material.

Week Four: Day Two

What Does the New Testament Say About Homosexuality?

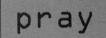

God knows everything about you: every thought, every victory and strength, every weakness and failure. He knows every quirk of your personality and every desire you've ever had. Even still, He is here beside you now, waiting to meet with you. He always arrives before you, desiring to connect with you even more than your closest friend. **Take a moment to greet your loving God.**

Yesterday you learned that the Old Testament is very clear about God's view of homosexual activities. But what does the New Testament say?

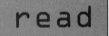

Read Romans 1:26–27, and as you do look for the answer to this question: Why is homosexual behavior immoral? **Use the space below to write your answer.**

_____

_____

_____

In Romans 1:26–27 the apostle Paul (who wrote this book of the Bible) declared both male homosexuality and female homosexuality (lesbianism) to be immoral because it is unnatural. That's the answer to the question: _homosexuality is wrong because it is unnatural._ But what does that mean? And why is homosexuality unnatural? **If you did not include this in your answer above, then look carefully at the passage again (especially verse 27) and use the space below to describe why Paul insisted that homosexuality was unnatural.**

_____

_____

_____

In Romans 1:27 Paul indicates that God's intention for sex is that it should be between a man and a woman. Only sex between a man and a woman is natural, because this alone fits God's design, God's purpose, God's plan.

God alone, as the Creator of all things, including humans and sex, has the right to determine the rules for sexual activity. And God designed you to have sex only with your wife. Therefore, homosexual activities are "unnatural" (literally "against nature") because they are contrary to God's design for sex. In other words, to say that homosexual activity is "unnatural" is to say that it is not natural to God's plan for sex.

Read 1 Corinthians 6:9–11.

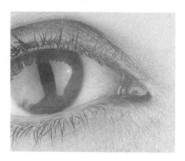

There are many different ways to translate the last phrase of verse 9: (The letters in parentheses are the abbreviations for particular Bible translations) *male sodomites* (NRSV); *male prostitutes* and *homosexual offenders* (NIV); *catamites* and *sodomites* (JB, Moffatt, and Barrett); *sexual perverts* (REB); *effeminate* and *homosexuals* (KJV, NASB, AV, RV); *male prostitutes* and *homosexuals* (NLT); *men who practice homosexuality* (ESV). The reason for so many different versions is because the words Paul uses are very difficult to translate from Greek (the original language of the New Testament) into English. However, while they do not always translate these phrases in the same way, most modern scholars agree on the main idea: Paul is addressing the two partners in a homosexual relationship—one person is passive while the other is active.

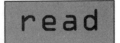
read

Now read 1 Corinthians 6:9–10 again. As you do, notice that Paul doesn't only condemn homosexuality; he also points to other types of sexual behavior. In the space below, list the four different types of sexual sin that Paul describes.

_____

_____

_____

_____

_____

_____

Two of these sins are heterosexual sins, and two are homosexual sins. The heterosexual sins are: fornication (sexual immorality) and adultery. Fornication means sex between unmarried people—for example, two teenagers "hooking up." Adultery, on the other hand, is any type of sexual activity between a married person and someone they are not married to—for example, having an affair with a married person. This is just one of the places in the Bible where you learn that fornication and adultery are sins just like homosexual activities. You see, the Bible doesn't simply "pick on" homosexuality. It regards homosexuality as a sexual sin, just like the other types of sexual sin that you have been studying throughout *Great Love.*

The Debate

In 1 Corinthians 6:9–11 Paul lists ten types of sinners that "will not inherit the kingdom of God" (verse 9). One of these is the person engaged in homosexual behavior. These verses teach that a Christian is someone who has surrendered to the lordship of Jesus Christ, and as a result, not only is that person forgiven of their sins, they are also commanded to surrender to the transforming power of the Holy Spirit, resulting in their freedom from a lifestyle of sin. This is Paul's main point: "Such were some of you" (verse 11). In other words, the mighty power of God has transformed you from your former life of sin. This does not mean that you will no longer struggle with old temptations. It means that through the power of the Holy Spirit you are being transformed into a person who resists these temptations. The focus of this passage is on habitual behavior.

The Bottom Line

So, the Bible clearly condemns homosexual behavior. Based upon the passages that you've looked at yesterday and today, you can see that all types of homosexual behavior are condemned as wickedness. This includes, among other things, homosexual rape, homosexual child abuse, and consensual homosexual sex between committed "partners." Both the Old Testament and the New Testament are clear in their condemnation of homosexual behavior: it is a sin. In the Old Testament the sin of homosexual behavior was punishable by death. However, things changed in the New Testament. (For example, see Acts 10:9–33, where God told Peter that the Old Testament food laws were no longer in effect.) The command to execute those who commit acts of homosexuality is no longer in effect. However, the New Testament makes it clear that homosexual acts are still considered sinful.

When it comes to homosexuality, a person faces the same choice that has been emphasized throughout *Great Love*: will you accept God's plan for your life? As a Christian you are supposed to let Christ be the Lord of every aspect of your life—including your sexual desires. Will you surrender to His plan for your sexual behavior? Being a Christian means that you surrender to God's will. It means that you humbly ask: "What is God's truth? With the help of God's power I will follow Him, no matter how difficult that is."

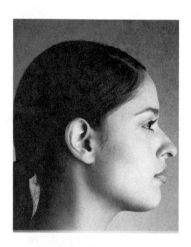

How are you reacting to this material? Are you challenged? Comforted? Angry? Confused? Sad? Imagine that Jesus Christ is standing or sitting across from you. For the next few minutes be honest with Him. **Speak out your feelings as one trusted friend to another.**

Week Four: Day Three

How Should Christians Treat a Person with Homosexual Desires?

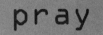

Colossians 1:16–17 describes Christ: "For by Him all things were created...all things have been created through Him and for Him.... and in Him all things hold together." So, not only is God right there (wherever you are) waiting for you, He is at work holding you together. Close your eyes and "Be still" (Psalm 46:10). Slow down, calm down, until you are aware of the beating of your heart, the ebb and flow of your breathing. These are signs of God's presence in your life. **Now thank God for His faithful presence, and ask Him to open your heart to receive His Word today.**

On July 7, 1984, in Bangor, Maine, a gang of guys attacked Charlie Howard, a 23-year-old man, because he was identified as a homosexual. Charlie begged for his life, but they refused to show mercy. They finally threw him from a bridge, killing him. On the night of October 6–7, 1998, two men attacked Matthew Shepherd because of his homosexual lifestyle. They beat him so severely that he passed out and never regained consciousness, finally dying from his injuries within a few days. From a Christian perspective, what is wrong with this kind of behavior? **Record your ideas in the space below.**

_____

_____

_____

_____

_____

Great Love for Guys

At Matthew Shepherd's funeral, a group of people who claimed to be Christians waved signs that read "God Hates Fags." From a Christian perspective, what is wrong with this kind of behavior? **Record your ideas in the space below.**

_____

_____

_____

_____

_____

_____

_____

_____

The Bible is clear, from the first book (Genesis) to the last book (Revelation), that one of the key tests for authentic Christianity is how you treat the needy and the social outcasts. **Read Exodus 22:21–27, Matthew 25:31–46, and James 1:27.** As you do, identify some of the reasons that God wants you to be kind to people who are looked down upon and not treated fairly by the rest of the world. **Use the space below to record these reasons.**

| read |

_____

_____

_____

_____

_____

_____

_____

_____

Use the space below to list some of the ways that people today mistreat those who engage in the homosexual lifestyle. Don't forget to include all types of mistreatment, including physical, verbal, psychological, and social.

_____

_____

_____

_____

Did you include gay jokes that are common, even in many Christian youth groups? Things like acting as if you are gay by talking with a lisp or having a limp wrist? What about using slang terms such as "light in the loafers," "floaters," "queer," "fag," "lesbo," "dyke," "butch," etc.? Even if no one is getting hurt (which is something that you can never really know), this is terribly inappropriate because you are making light of a sin that God strongly disapproves of. To have fun by imitating something that God says is bad enough to be called a sin is wrong.

| read |

Read Colossians 3:5–6. In this passage, what is the cause of God's wrath? **Use the space below to record your answer.**

_____

_____

_____

_____

Depending on the version of the Bible that you are reading, you should have written something like: those who practice sexual immorality, impurity, lustful passion, evil desire, and greed.

Now read the next two verses (Colossians 3:7–8). What do verses 7–8 add to the list of sins that will bring God's wrath?

read

_____

_____

_____

_____

Depending on the version of the Bible that you are reading, you should have written something like: anger, wrath, malice, slander, and obscene talk (or abusive speech). Pretty intense, isn't it? God ranks "anger" and "abusive speech" right up there with "sexual immorality." **What does this mean regarding the behavior of the group of so-called "Christians" at the funeral of Matthew Shepherd?**

_____

_____

_____

_____

Colossians 3:5–8 teaches that Christians must never be mean to anyone, including those who identify themselves as homosexual. To attack such a person physically, verbally, psychologically, or socially is absolutely inexcusable. Not only should you refuse to act in such ways, you should also take a stand against this type of behavior when others are doing it. To be like Jesus means you are supposed to insist on fair treatment for everyone. Have you ever witnessed someone being picked on, made fun of, mistreated, or laughed at because they were (or appeared to be) homosexual? **What did you do?**

_____

_____

_____

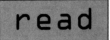**read**

You've looked at some ways that Christians should *not* treat others. But what are some ways that Christians *should* treat those who identify themselves as homosexuals, or who are struggling with homosexual desires and attractions? **Read the following passages of Scripture to see how Jesus treated the sexual sinners of His day.**

John 4:7–27—The woman in this passage had been married five times (verses 17–18) and was currently living with a man she wasn't married to. The people in her city thought so little of her that she had to go to the well (to draw water) in the middle of the day, the hottest part of the day, by herself. Notice how Jesus treats this woman who was considered an outcast because of her many divorces. **In the space below, summarize Jesus' attitude toward this woman.**

_____

_____

_____

_____

_____

John 8:1–11—According to the Old Testament, this woman deserved to be executed because she committed adultery. The men in the community wanted to follow through with the sentence. **In the space below, describe how you think this woman felt about Jesus when the whole experience was over.**

_____

_____

_____

_____

_____

Matthew 11:18–19—The religious leaders were very angry that Jesus was nice to people who were guilty of the worst sins (according to the religious leaders), and these especially included sexual sins. As a result, they gave Jesus a nickname, a name that they hated. In fact, it was one of the worst names that a religious person could ever call someone. They called Jesus: "A friend of tax-collectors and sinners."

Luke 15—Jesus eventually earned a reputation, both with the religious leaders and with those who were outcasts because of their sins. In verses 1–2 you see that the "bad" people loved hanging out with Jesus. In fact, they were drawn to Him like a magnet. But the religious leaders hated this and made fun of Him. You can hear the anger, sarcasm, and arrogance dripping from their words as they whisper to one another: "Look at Jesus, he even eats with the filthy sinners!"

Use the space below to describe what you think all of these glimpses into the life of Jesus mean for how you should treat those who identify themselves as homosexuals or who are struggling with homosexual desires. (Remember, Jesus was clear about the fact that homosexuality was sinful. The Bible is not contradicting itself on this subject.)

_____

_____

_____

_____

_____

Since God chose you to be the holy people whom he loves, you must clothe yourselves with tender-hearted mercy, kindness, humility, gentleness, and patience. You must make allowance for each other's faults and forgive the person who offends you. Remember, the Lord forgave you, so you must forgive others. And the most important piece of clothing you must wear is love. Love is what binds us all together in perfect harmony. And let the peace that comes from Christ rule in your hearts. For as members of one body you are all called to live in peace. And always be thankful.
—Colossians 3:12–15 (NLT)

Read Colossians 3:12–15. (It's in the margin.)

read

This passage is speaking mainly about how Christians should treat other Christians. However, it also applies to how Christians should treat even those who are not Christian. Christians should form friendships with people who engage in homosexual activities even though their lifestyles and behaviors are sinful. You should be "tender-hearted" and full of "mercy, kindness, humility, gentleness, and patience." The bottom line: you must act with love. Jesus is your model in this. He had great relationships with the "immoral" and "sinful" people in His day. He would visit them in their homes, eat with them, and spend time with them.

You can follow in Jesus' footsteps by loving and valuing homosexuals as people whom God loves and values. Can you think of a person you know of who identifies himself or herself as homosexual or who is struggling with homosexual desires? **Use the space below to record three specific ways that you can show this person the love of Jesus through your actions.**

_____

_____

_____

_____

_____

_____

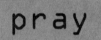 Reflect on what you have learned. You have learned that sexual immorality (whether it is heterosexual or homosexual) will bring the wrath of God. You've also learned that anger and mean words will bring the wrath of God. Are you guilty of mistreating (physically, verbally, emotionally, or socially) those who struggle with homosexual desires? Do you need to honestly confess a sin? Do you need to plead for mercy? Do you need to ask God to break your heart over your sin, because your heart is cold and hard to the wickedness of your own iniquity? Do you know of someone who is struggling with this issue that you can form a real friendship with? For the next few moments, sit before the Lord. Imagine that He is standing or sitting in front of you. **Speak with Him about these things and listen as He speaks to you.**

Week Four: Day Four

The Difference Between Temptation and Sin

Before Jesus died, He prayed for His disciples. Part of that prayer is printed below.

pray

As you begin today's session, imagine that Jesus Christ is sitting across from you. Read His prayer slowly and prayerfully, and hear Jesus praying to God on your behalf.

> *But now I come to You; and these things I speak in the world so that they may have My joy made full in themselves. I have given them Your word; and the world has hated them, because they are not of the world, even as I am not of the world. I do not ask You to take them out of the world, but to keep them from the evil one. They are not of the world, even as I am not of the world. Sanctify them in the truth; Your word is truth. As You sent Me into the world, I also have sent them into the world. For their sakes I sanctify Myself, that they themselves also may be sanctified in truth.*
>
> *I do not ask on behalf of these alone, but for those also who believe in Me through their word; that they may all be one; even as You, Father, are in Me and I in You, that they also may be in Us, so that the world may believe that You sent Me. The glory which You have given Me I have given to them, that they may be one, just as We are one; I in them and You in Me, that they may be perfected in unity, so that the world may know that You sent Me, and loved them, even as You have loved Me.*
> —John 17:13–23

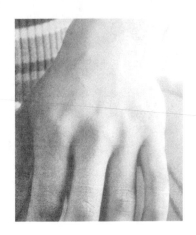

God created you as a sexual being, so your desire for sex is a gift from God. However, from the moment that Adam and Eve gave in to the temptation of the serpent (Genesis 3), all of creation has been deeply wounded. Albert Wolters, in his book *Creation Regained,* shows that the Bible teaches that the sin of Adam and Eve was not some little bitty sin but was "an event of catastrophic significance" for every square inch of creation. This includes all humans and even every non-human part of God's creation. Just one example of the terrible effects of sin is that your God-given desire for sex is perverted into lust; that is, you have a desire for sexual experiences that God does not approve of.

Part of what this means is that God did not create adultery, fornication, lust, pornography, or homosexual desires. God creates humans with a sex drive, but sin and the devil pervert the sex drive that God has given you. For some people this results in the desire for lustful thoughts, sex outside of marriage, or homosexual experiences. You see, the temptations to look at pornography, to lust, and to fool around with your girlfriend are just like the temptations of homosexual attractions, urges, desires, and longings. Whether your temptations are heterosexual or homosexual, you are still facing the temptation of sexual immorality.

But did you know that the Bible teaches that temptation is different from sin? Did you know that *temptation is not sin*? Temptation becomes sin the moment you act on it (either mentally or physically). If you feel the urge to have sexual thoughts about someone (no matter what gender they are), it is a temptation. But if you continue to think about that urge and imagine yourself carrying out that urge— that is sin. So when you feel the urge, it is your response that determines if you enter into sin or not. To sin is to dwell on the desire, to feed it, to imagine it, to do it. But if you dismiss it through prayer, faith, and by the power of the Holy Spirit, then you have defeated temptation; you have not sinned.

read

Read Matthew 4:1–11. Who is being tempted in this passage?

_____

Great Love for Guys

Read Hebrews 4:14–15.

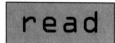

In these verses, you learn that Jesus was tempted just like you are. However, it says that Jesus did not sin. Clearly then, to be tempted is not the same thing as being guilty of sin.

You are not responsible for your temptations, but you are responsible for your response to temptation.

You are not judged for your temptations, but you are judged for your response to temptation.

Now think about how this applies to your life. When you are walking down the hall at school and you see an attractive person, it is not a sin to feel that attraction. However, it is a sin to allow yourself to be carried away by lust. For example, when a girl bends down to pick up a pencil, and her shirt falls open, and you can see her breast—if you notice this and are tempted to look down her shirt, and you want to, *that desire to look is not the sin*. But if you give in to that desire and actually stare down her shirt, then you have crossed the line—you have sinned. It becomes sin when you give in to the temptation, or when you allow those erotic thoughts to continue to play in the theater of your mind. **Use the space below to describe, in your own words, the difference between temptation and sin.**

> No temptation has overtaken you that is not common to man. God is faithful, and he will not let you be tempted beyond your ability, but with the temptation he will also provide the way of escape, that you may be able to endure it.
> —1 Corinthians 10:13
> (ESV)

_____

_____

_____

_____

_____

Read 1 Corinthians 10:13. (It's in the margin.)

read

Use the space below to describe what does this passage teaches you about temptation, about God, and about your response to temptation.

_____

_____

_____

_____

_____

_____

_____

pray

Imagine that Jesus is standing or sitting in front of you. **Have an honest, open conversation with Him about what you are feeling or thinking in response to today's material.**

Week Four: Day Five

Great Hope

pray

Remember the image from Saint Ignatius—the bland and shapeless tree trunk. Remember the picture of the artist shaping it with the chisel. Remember that the artist could see the beautiful sculpture that the tree trunk could become. As you begin today's session, reflect upon all of the shaping (the chiseling, chipping, and cutting) that God has done with you on your journey through *Great Love*. Take a moment to reflect upon God's work in your life and praise Him for this.

Congratulations!

You've made it to the end of *Great Love.* What a ride! The fact that you've made it this far shows that God is at work in your life right now. He's been leading you through His Word, into prayer, and to truth. Once again, *congratulations*!

But let's be honest. If you're human, there is a chance that you are still struggling with some issues of sexual temptation (whether it is sex outside of marriage, lust, pornography, or homosexual desires). It would be nice if your sexual impulses were automatically adjusted to God's standard the minute you surrendered to God's plan. Wouldn't that be cool? The Holy Spirit would cause your lustful desires to vanish the moment you were saved. But that's not how it usually works. However, don't fear, because *there is hope!* Remember that many, many people have experienced victory in this battle. If you are willing to pursue obedience and devotion to Christ, then you can find freedom from the bondage of sexual immorality through the unconditional love and grace of God.

It probably won't be easy, though. To be completely honest, letting God deliver you from sexual immorality may be the most difficult experience that you ever endure. The call to be holy in your sex life is very challenging—especially in our sin-sick, sexually perverted society. But God offers you a plan for victory. You've been learning about this plan throughout *Great Love.* So it will be good to end this entire study by looking at a passage of Scripture that wraps up a lot of what you've been experiencing.

Read James 4:5–10. (It's in the margin.)

This is not an easy passage of Scripture to understand. However, when you do understand it, you will see that it is simply awesome! First of all, look in verses 7–9 and discover five basic actions that can help you experience victory in the war that Satan has declared on you. **List these actions below.**

1. S_____ to God. (verse 7)

⁵Or do you suppose it is to no purpose that the Scripture says, "He yearns jealously over the spirit that he has made to dwell in us"? ⁶But he gives more grace. Therefore it says, "God opposes the proud, but gives grace to the humble." ⁷Submit yourselves therefore to God. Resist the devil, and he will flee from you. ⁸Draw near to God, and he will draw near to you. Cleanse your hands, you sinners, and purify your hearts, you double-minded. ⁹Be wretched and mourn and weep. Let your laughter be turned to mourning and your joy to gloom. ¹⁰Humble yourselves before the Lord, and he will exalt you.
—James 4:5–10 (ESV)

read

2. R_____ the Devil. (verse 7)

3. D_____ near to G_____. (verse 8)

4. C_____ my hands and p_____ my heart. (verse 8)

5. Be wretched and m_____ and w_____. Let my l_____ be turned into mourning and my j_____ to g_____. (verse 9)

All five actions are crucial for finding hope and forgiveness.

Action 1: Submit—You've been challenged to do this since the first day of *Great Love*. Over and over again you've faced this basic issue: will you trust that God is good and accept His plan for your life? To do this is to surrender to God, to submit your life and your plans and your desires to His will.

Action 2: Resist—Again, you've discovered a ton of practical ways to resist Satan's attack.

Action 3: Draw Near—Every session began and ended with directions for you to pray and open yourself up to God's presence.

Action 4: Cleanse and Purify—Day after day and week after week, you were challenged to turn from old habits, to stop doing the things that displeased God, to confess your own sinfulness. You were urged to give your heart and mind fully to God and God alone!

Action 5: Mourn and Weep—You were given plenty of opportunities to be truly broken over any sin that was in your life.

Now take your time to go through this book, and evaluate the impact of each section on your life according to these five steps. In other words, as you flip through Week One ("How to Have Sex Before You Get Married") ask yourself these questions:

1. Are there any aspects of God's plan that I discovered in those sessions that I still haven't accepted?
2. Are there any practical ideas for resisting Satan's attack that I have not put into practice?
3. Did I take the prayer times at the beginning and end of each session seriously? Did I slow down and actually focus on God? Did I listen for His voice, and look for His work in my life as I studied His Word? Did I truly seek after God as I studied the material, or did I just go through the motions?
4. Have I continued to turn away from the things that displease God? Have I continued to fight for putting God at the center of my heart?
5. Was I honest enough to admit that my sin is truly wicked? Did I genuinely mourn over and confess any sins that this lesson pointed out in my life?

After doing this for Week One, do the same thing for Week Two. Open yourself up to God's presence. Listen closely for the gentle nudging of His Holy Spirit. **Use the space below to record any unfinished business for each week.**

Week One

_____

_____

_____

_____

_____

Week Two

_____

_____

_____

_____

_____

_____

Week Three

_____

_____

_____

_____

_____

_____

Week Four

_____

_____

_____

_____

_____

_____

Go back and read James 4:5–6 one more time.

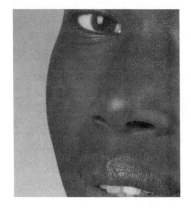

In verse 5 you are told that God "yearns jealously over the spirit that he has made to dwell in us." This is really good news. It means that if you are a Christian, God has put the Holy Spirit in you, and God is very protective of His Spirit. He doesn't give the Holy Spirit to just anybody. Oh no! He only gives the Holy Spirit to His children, to Christians. So you see, His jealousy is a good thing. It means that because the Holy Spirit is in you, then God is definitely on your side. He is in your corner, cheering you on. He has a stake in this matter, and He is working to make sure that you succeed. That's why verse 6 says that God has given you "more grace." He's giving you more of His goodness so that you can be victorious. As you continue to surrender to His plan, He continues to pour His goodness into your life. Verses 5–6 teach you that God is on your side and will continue to give you His grace (His goodness, strength, courage, forgiveness, etc.) so that you will be victorious. Wow! What an amazing privilege. Because of the death and resurrection of Jesus Christ, God (the Holy Spirit) is in you, and therefore God (the Father) is going to make sure that you succeed!

But there's more. James 4:5–6 also points out that there is something you can do so that God will increase the supply of grace that comes into your life. When verse 6 says, "God opposes the proud, but gives grace to the humble," it teaches a very important lesson. Imagine that God's grace is like water flowing out of the showerhead. When you turn the handle one way, the water flows out stronger and stronger. But when you turn the handle the other way, the flow of water slows down until there is none coming out. Well, James 4:6 shows you that when you humble yourself before God, it is like turning the faucet on full blast so that more and more of God's grace can flow into your life.

read

So how do you humble yourself before God? Actually, you already know the answer to that question. It's the five actions that you found in verses 7–9. You listed them earlier. **Look closely again James 4:5–10** (it's printed in the margin at the front of week 4, day 5). **Circle the two times that the word "humble" appears.**

Did you circle the last word of verse 6 and the first word of verse 10? Verse 6 says that if you want more grace from God you've got to be humble. Verses 7–9 give some really practical ways to be humble. Finally, verse 10 tells you to get on with business and humble yourself. In other words, verse 6 says that humility is the key to more grace. Verses 7–9 tell you how to be humble. Then verse 10 says, "So what are you waiting for? Humble yourself!"

One more thing. Look at verse 10. Do you see that last phrase? ("and he will exalt you.") It's awesome to think that as you humble yourself (submit, resist, draw near, cleanse, purify, and mourn), God will pour His grace into your life by lifting you up above temptation so that you are victorious!

pray

In these final moments, talk with God about whatever He is provoking within you. Imagine Jesus standing or sitting beside you. **Open your heart to Him as you share and listen.**

As you finish your time today, recite "The Doxology": *Glory be to the Father, and to the Son, and to the Holy Spirit; as it was in the beginning, is now, and ever shall be, world without end. Amen.*

Conclusion

Sex is a great gift from a great God who loves you with a great love! That's what this entire Bible study has been about. But the end of this study doesn't have to be the end of your adventure with God. While the specific purpose of this book has centered on the issue of sexual purity, the larger goal has been an invitation for you to experience the joy of a relationship with your Creator. After all, that really is the key to having a great sex life.

This is not meant to give you the impression that if you do everything found in this book, if you dedicate yourself to following Jesus Christ, then you are guaranteed to have an awesome sex life. In fact, there is much more to it than you've discovered here. This material has been written merely to give you a vision for waiting until you are married before you begin that wonderful journey, with your wife, into the joys, pleasures, and satisfaction of sexual intimacy. On the other hand, by following God's plan you will be on the right track to experience the greatness of sex as God intended it.

Obviously, this is not an easy route to take. All of hell is assembled against you. But the opposite is also true: all of heaven is cheering you on! That's what the writer of Hebrews says:

Therefore, since we are surrounded by so great a cloud of witnesses, let us also lay aside every weight, and sin which clings so closely, and let us run with endurance the race that is set before us, looking to Jesus, the founder and perfecter of our faith, who for the joy that was set before him endured the cross, despising the shame, and is seated at the right hand of the throne of God.
—Hebrews 12:1–2 (ESV)

Because of "the joy set before him," Jesus was able to endure the cross and the shame. That's the key to your success. Keep focusing on Jesus. Keep diving into your relationship with Him. Keep listening for His voice, seeking His presence, and sharing your heart with Him. And as you do this, remember God has a *great love* for you. And out of His great love He has given humanity the gift of sex. Hang in there. Wait on God's timing. Trust that His way is the best way. Trust that the joy He offers you is really the best joy.

Session Guidelines for the Leader

Dear leader, this guide is provided to help you lead your small group in the study of *Great Love*. First of all, be sure you allow time for the students to speak up and share their thoughts—even if this means there are short periods of silence while they gather their thoughts. It's okay! The guys in your group may be slow to speak out. However, as they become more comfortable with the material and with the group, this will change.

Second, always remember that small groups can be a wonderful time of fellowship. Make it fun, welcome everyone and keep the discussion positive. Don't allow judgmental comments or gossip to become a part of this time. Be sure to let everyone have an opportunity to share—being careful not to let one or two guys dominate the discussion.

Thirdly, and perhaps most importantly, your job is to pray. Pray for your own knowledge and spiritual growth, as well as for each of your students, by name, each day. Be sensitive to the guidance of the Holy Spirit when leading your group. Each group is unique and you should ask the Lord's insight into the direction He wants your group to go each week.

Remember, these are simply suggestion to help you get started. God will bless you with wisdom because of your willingness to lead and teach His Truth. And the students are sure to grow in their knowledge and faith as you listen to His Word together.

In preparation:
Prayerfully and thoughtfully complete all five days of the session. During your daily time with *Great Love*, jot down any ideas or possible discussion questions that come to mind. Your personal experience

with God through *Great Love* will be a very important aspect of preparation for the group time. Then, before your group meeting, take some time to look back over each day's material for that week. As you do:

- Pray, asking for the Holy Spirit to guide you toward those issues that are most important for your group.
- Be sure to note the most crucial points for each day. Prepare to lead a discussion that helps the students to really dig deep into these key issues.
- Be prayed up and right with God, so that you can be used as a vessel for Him to work through.

Let's begin!

Week 1: How to Have Sex Before You Get Married

Welcome
Offer a warm and joyful welcome to your group.

Ice Breaker (5 minutes)
Introduce yourself and then have the guys introduce themselves. Be creative and use some fun way to break the ice.

Group Discussion (35 minutes)
Have some of your students read Proverbs 7 aloud to the group.
Use the following for discussion starters:

- "Let's see if we can remember the six steps that lead to sexual immorality. Without looking in your copy of *Great Love,* call out the steps that you remember."
- "Now look back through your book, and share with the group some statements in the workbook that were particularly important to you."
- "Are there any other areas or issues that you would like to discuss?"
- "What did God say to you as you worked through Week One?"
- "What changes do you sense the Lord Jesus asking you to make?"
- "Would someone like to share a prayer you wrote or voice an area you struggle with?"
- "Does anyone have any other thoughts that God brought to mind this week as you listened to His voice through His Word?"

Prayer (15 minutes)
One of the most powerful things that you can experience through this study is the opportunity to pray with other Christians about these issues. Each week we will spend some time doing just that, praying together.

Leader, every group is different. With a Spirit-given sensitivity, choose an option for leading your group through the prayer time.

You could:

- Break the guys into pairs or groups of three to have them share and pray for each other.
- Get in a large circle and have each guy pray a sentence prayer.
- Pray for them yourself.

Closing (5 minutes)

- Prepare the group by creating anticipation for the next week's study.
- Encourage them to continue their time with Jesus each day.
- Challenge them to be diligent in completing their assignments daily.
- Let them know that you will be praying for them during the next week.
- Make sure they know where and when your next small group time will be.

Week 2: How to Avoid Having Sex Before You Get Married

Welcome

Offer a warm and joyful welcome to your group. Have someone pray for your group out loud for the time together that you are about to have.

Group Discussion (40 minutes)

- Have someone read Proverbs 7:1–5.
- Say, "On Day Two and Day Three, you studied three ways that we are commanded to treat God's plan. Without looking in your book, call out those three ways." Have the students briefly, and in their own words, explain each.
- Have someone read Proverbs 7:22–27.
- Say, "On Day Four and Day Five, you studied the two components of God's plan for avoiding sexual immorality. What are the two things that you must do if you want to be sexually pure?" Again,

have the students briefly, and in their own words, explain each.

- Have the students look back through their books and share with the group some statements or activities in the workbook that were particularly important to them.
- If the students did not bring up the whole issue of choosing to accept God's plan (the most important decision that we face in *Great Love*) bring it up now and lead a discussion around it. Perhaps ask them, "Did you make the choice to accept God's plan?"
- Ask, "What did God say to you as you worked through Week Two?"
- Ask, "What changes do you sense the Lord Jesus asking you to make?"
- Ask, "Does anyone have any other thoughts that God brought to mind this week as you listened to His voice through His Word?"

Prayer (15 minutes)
With a Spirit-given sensitivity, choose an option for leading your group through the prayer time. You could:
- Break the guys into pairs or groups of three to have them share and pray for each other.
- Get in a large circle and have each guy pray a sentence prayer.
- Pray for them yourself.

Closing (5 minutes)
- Prepare the group by creating anticipation for the next week's study.
- Encourage them to continue their time with Jesus each day.
- Challenge them to be diligent in completing their assignments daily.
- Let them know that you will be praying for them during the next week.
- Make sure they know where and when your next small group time will be.

Illustration: Marinate
Get two pieces of chicken, two baggies, and some seasoning salt or other marinade. Marinate one of the pieces of chicken all day to bring to the group. Do not marinate the other piece of chicken.

Compare the differences with your group: the smell, the craving, the difference in appearance, etc. Use this to show that when we marinate in the things of God we are different, we look different, people want what we have; once we get a taste of the good stuff we began to crave it.

Week 3: God's Plan for Great Dating

Welcome

Be sure to offer a warm and joyful welcome to your group. Have someone pray for your group out loud for the time together that you are about to have.

Group Discussion (40 minutes)

Use the following for discussion starters:

- "Isn't it amazing that we can hear God speaking to us today through the story in Genesis 3 of Adam and Eve? What significant lesson in their story can you relate to your dating life?"
- "Let's talk about how important it is to surrender to God's plan even when we don't understand it or like it."
- "Why should looking first to God to satisfy us be such a huge priority?"
- "What is the difference between a Christian girl and a sold-out Christian girl?" Be sure to read the Scriptures that support the various answers given.
- "What are some of the qualities that you listed in your book regarding your expectations for your future wife?"
- "What are the 3 basic steps to dating in a way that pleases God?"
- "What did God say to you as you worked through Week Three?"
- "What changes do you sense the Lord Jesus asking you to make?"
- "What were the highlights of this week's material for you?"
- "Does anyone have any other thoughts that God brought to mind this week as you listened to His voice through His Word?"

Prayer (15 minutes)

Lead the students to talk about the image of the tree trunk that Saint Ignatius presented. Be sure to mention how wonderful it is to know that God loves us with His Great Love! He's not finished working on us, shaping us into the unique and strong young men that He created us to be. This is good news!

With a Spirit-given sensitivity, choose an option for leading your group through the prayer time. You could:
- Break the guys into pairs or groups of three to have them share and pray for each other.
- Get in a large circle and have each guy pray a sentence prayer.
- Pray for them yourself.

Closing (5 minutes)
- Prepare the group by creating anticipation for the next week's study.
- Encourage them to continue their time with Jesus each day.
- Challenge them to be diligent in completing their assignments daily.
- Let them know that you will be praying for them during the next week.
- Make sure they know where and when your next small group time will be.

Week 4: What Does God Say About Homosexuality & Conclusion to Great Love

Welcome
Be sure to offer a warm and joyful welcome to your group. Have someone pray out loud for the time together that you are about to have.

Group Discussion (40 minutes)
Use the following for discussion starters:
- "How many movies and popular prime time TV shows can you name that have homosexuals as main characters?"
- "What kind of impact do you think this has on you and your friends?"
- "How many of you know someone who is gay?" (Don't allow them to give names.)

- "What did you learn this week about what the Bible says about homosexuality?" Be sure to read some of the passages as you talk about them.
- "You looked at several passages of Scripture that make it clear that we should show compassion and kindness toward people who have homosexual feelings. What can you do to reflect Jesus (1) to those who live the homosexual lifestyle, or (2) to those who hate the person who lives a homosexual lifestyle? Has this week's lesson helped you know how to better respond? What particular statements were important to you?"
- "Now let's shift gears and focus on the last two days of *Great Love* Week Four. Look back over Days Four and Five. What are some statements or activities that were particularly important to you?"
- "Are there any other areas or issues that you would like to discuss?"
- "What did God say to you as you worked through Week Four?"
- "What changes do you sense the Lord Jesus asking you to make?"
- "Would someone like to share a prayer you wrote or voice an area you struggle with?"
- "Does anyone have any other thoughts that God brought to mind this week as you listened to His voice through His Word?"

Note: It may be good to end *Great Love* with a discussion around the following questions.
- "How can you make a difference?"
- "Will you share what you have learned with your friends?"

Prayer (15 minutes)

Give everyone a chance to share brokenness, joy, forgiveness, and excitement as they look at praying for their future mate, prayer needs, struggles, their fresh relationship with God, the intimacy they now have, the changes they have already made, and challenges before them.

With a Spirit-given sensitivity, choose an option for leading your group through the prayer time. You could:

- Break the guys into pairs or groups of three to have them share and pray for each other.
- Get in a large circle and have each guy pray a sentence prayer.
- Pray for them yourself.

Closing (5 minutes)

Has there been a time in your life where you went ahead with something before you had all the instructions and it didn't turn out right? (Examples: putting together a bike, installing something electronic, cooking something, etc.) This is why it is so important to know God's plan, and to be patient while He molds us and shapes us. Many times we try to rush it so we can see the results. Just like the putting together a bike—if you don't put all the parts in the right place, or you rush the assembly and don't read the instructions, your bike could end up looking pretty funny and not working right. You see, we too must be patient and let God to reveal His plan for our lives each day. If we rush it, chances are we won't like what we see. If we rush it, we will be disappointed. If we rush it, we can become emotionally scarred and sometimes physically scarred for the rest of our lives. In addition, when we rush it we may miss out on some good things God had planned for us.

- Encourage them to continue their time with Jesus each day.
- Let them know that you will be praying for them during the weeks ahead. Make sure they know they can contact you any time concerning accountability, prayer needs, or anything else.
- Have your group say the "Doxology" together (found at the end of Week Four).

Note:
- This closing session doesn't have to be the end at all. Now that you have become close as a group, you may decide to choose another study and continue your small group time.
- Fellowship is important and the memories these guys have made will impact their lives for years to come. Celebrate with a party. Have fun!

Also by Chandra Peele

Discovering true love, beauty, and confidence

by Chandra Peele

Foreword by Max Lucado

1-56309-909-8

Priceless
Discovering True Love, Beauty, and Confidence

A six-week interactive Bible study to help teen girls know that they are priceless—and that their best self is found in relationship with Jesus.

Available in bookstores everywhere.

new
hope
PUBLISHERS

Inspiring Women. Changing Lives.